SALVATION

SALVATION

How Christ Brings Us to Life

ROBERT L. REYMOND

Reformation Heritage Books
Grand Rapids, Michigan

Reformation Heritage Books
3070 29th St. SE
Grand Rapids, MI 49512
616–977–0889
orders@heritagebooks.org
www.heritagebooks.org

Unless otherwise indicated, Scripture taken from the New King James Version®. Copyright © 1982 by Thomas Nelson. Used by permission. All rights reserved.

Scripture marked KJV taken from the King James Version. In the public domain.

All italics in Scripture quotations have been added.

Portions of this work are taken from *A New Systematic Theology of the Christian Faith* by Robert L. Reymond. Copyright © 1998 by Thomas Nelson, Inc. by permission of HarperCollins Christian Publishing. www.harpercollinschristian.com

Printed in the United States of America
25 26 27 28 29 30/10 9 8 7 6 5 4 3 2 1

Library of Congress Cataloging-in-Publication Data

Names: Reymond, Robert L., author.
Title: Salvation : how Christ brings us to life / Robert L. Reymond.
Description: Grand Rapids, Michigan : Reformation Heritage Books, [2025] |
    Includes bibliographical references.
Identifiers: LCCN 2024058531 (print) | LCCN 2024058532 (ebook) |
    ISBN 9798886861808 (paperback) | ISBN 9798886861815 (epub)
Subjects: LCSH: Salvation—Christianity.
Classification: LCC BT751.3 .R49 2025 (print) | LCC BT751.3 (ebook) |
    DDC 234—dc23/eng/20250108
LC record available at https://lccn.loc.gov/2024058531
LC ebook record available at https://lccn.loc.gov/2024058532

Contents

Foreword

No topic is more worthy of our attention than *salvation*. This is the great concern of human beings: how to live forever in perfect happiness. And this is the great end to which we are to live, for God saves sinners "to the praise of the glory of his grace" (Eph. 1:6 KJV).

This book on salvation represents an unusual fusion of the thought of two great Christian divines who were born nearly a century apart: Baptist preacher Charles Spurgeon (1834–1892) and Reformed theologian Robert Reymond (1932–2013). As Reymond wrote in the preface of another of his manuscripts, "I have read literally hundreds of Spurgeon's sermons for my own spiritual edification and the sheer joy they bring to my heart." He added, "What I have done here is to take…Spurgeon's sermons…and to convert them from their sermonic style… supplementing and contemporizing them where I felt it appropriate."

But Reymond did not merely edit Spurgeon's sermons for this book, but skillfully wove together Spurgeon's heart-stirring biblical eloquence with his own insightful Reformed theological teachings, as set forth in his highly regarded book, *A New Systematic Theology of the Christian Faith*. The result is "a burning and a shining light" (John 5:35 KJV) concerning the doctrine of salvation, a fit instrument for God to use by His grace to both illuminate the mind with knowledge and ignite the heart with love.

Having passed the tenth anniversary of Reymond's entrance into Christ's presence, we commend this book to you with the prayer that God will use it to begin the work of glory in you and lead you safely into the kingdom.

—Joel R. Beeke and Paul M. Smalley

Preface

These ten addresses on the application of Christ's atonement to God's chosen people, delivered at Holy Trinity Presbyterian Church in Fort Lauderdale, Florida, in 2009, presuppose Christ's accomplished work of atonement.[1] That is to say, they assume that when Christ lived His obedient life, died His sacrificial death on Calvary, and then rose bodily from the dead, He paid the penalty for His people's sins, enduring their curse and dying their death, thereby propitiating God's wrath against them; reconciling God to them; redeeming them from the curse of the law and the guilt, power, and fruitlessness of sin; and destroying the dark powers of the kingdom of evil, triumphing over it by His cross. Without Christ's mighty death work at Calvary, what I say in this book would be meaningless. But because Christ completed the work that His Father gave Him to do, crying from the cross, "It is finished" (John 19:30), and then three days later rising again from the dead, the church has a redemptive work, the benefits of which it can proclaim to humankind for their salvation. In sum, the whole system of Christianity rests on the life, death, and resurrection of Jesus Christ. John Calvin declared that our whole salvation is "comprehended in Christ":

> We should therefore take care not to derive the least portion of
> it from anywhere else. If we seek salvation, we are taught by the

---

1. See John Calvin, *Institutes of the Christian Religion*, ed. John T. McNeill, trans. Ford Lewis Battles, Library of Christian Classics (Philadelphia: Westminster, 1960), 2.15.17.

very name of Jesus that it is "of him." If we seek any other gifts of the Spirit, they will be found in his anointing. If we seek strength, it lies in his dominion; if purity, in his conception; if gentleness, it appears in his birth. For by his birth he was made like us in all respects that he might learn to feel our pain. If we seek redemption, it lies in his passion; if acquittal, in his condemnation; if remission of the curse, in his cross; if satisfaction, in his sacrifice; if purification, in his blood; if reconciliation, in his descent into hell; if mortification of the flesh, in his tomb; if newness of life, in his resurrection; if immortality, in the same; if inheritance of the Heavenly Kingdom, in his entrance into heaven; if protection, if security, if abundant supply of all blessings, in his Kingdom; if untroubled expectation of judgment, in the power given to him to judge. In short, since rich store of every kind of good abounds in him, let us drink our fill from his fountain, and from no other.[2]

This being so, the issue before us is, How does the elect sinner become a partaker of Christ's accomplishments at Calvary and at the tomb and become saved? It is a beautiful and orderly story, and I trust this book will prove beneficial to you.

A few words about this book's title, *Salvation*: The word *salvation* underscores deliverance from the guilt of all our sins. All of us have broken God's laws flagrantly; we have all wandered the downward road, though each has chosen a different way. Salvation brings to us the blotting out of all our horrible transgressions, acquittal from our criminality and our treason against the Most High, and purging from all guilt that we may stand accepted before the great Judge. Who in their right mind will deny that such salvation is an unspeakably desirable blessing?

But salvation means more than that; it includes *deliverance from the power of sin*. Our natural man is fond of evil, and we run after it greedily. We are the bondslaves of iniquity, and we love the bondage. This love of bondage is the worst aspect of our circumstances. But when salvation comes, it delivers people from the power of sin. They learn that sin is evil, and they regard it as such and loathe it. They repent that they were ever in love with it and turn their back on it.

---

2. Calvin, *Institutes*, 2.16.19.

They become, through God's Spirit, the master of their lusts, and they put their flesh beneath their feet and rise to the liberty of the children of God. Sadly, there are many who do not care for this; if this is salvation, they do not give a cent for it. They love their sins; they rejoice to follow the devices and imaginations of their corrupt hearts. Yet be assured: this emancipation from bad habits, unclean desires, and carnal passions is the main point in salvation, and if salvation does not deliver us from these, it is not and cannot be enjoyed by us. Dear reader, do you possess salvation from sin? Have you escaped the corruption that is in the world through lust? If not, you need to be deeply concerned about your own salvation.

Salvation also includes *deliverance from the present wrath of God* that abides on an unsaved person every moment of his or her life. Every person who is unforgiven is the minute-by-minute object of divine wrath. "God is a just judge, and God is angry with the wicked every day…. He bends His bow and makes it ready" (Ps. 7:11–12). To have God's arrow pointed at you every moment of your life, even though it fly not from the bow as yet, is a terrible thing. "He who does not believe is condemned already, because he has not believed in the name of the only begotten Son of God" (John 3:18). We are not on probation. In Adam we have already been found to be unworthy; we have already been weighed in the balances and found wanting. If you have not believed in Jesus, condemnation already rests on you. You are reprieved for a while, but your condemnation is assuredly recorded. Salvation, however, takes sinners from under the cloud of divine wrath and reveals to them the divine love. The saved person can then say,

> O LORD, I will praise You;
> Though You were angry with me,
> Your anger is turned away, and You comfort me. (Isa. 12:1)

Salvation at once sets us free from this frightful state of danger and alienation. We are no longer the "children of wrath, just as the others" (Eph. 2:3), but are made children of God and joint heirs with Christ Jesus. What can be more precious than this?

And then, last, we receive that part of salvation that some people mistakenly put first and make to be the whole of salvation. In consequence of our being delivered from the guilt and power of sin and from the present wrath of God, we are *delivered from the future wrath of God*. God's wrath will descend on the souls of non-Christians to the uttermost when they leave their bodies and stand before their Maker's bar if they depart this life without salvation. To die without salvation is to enter into damnation. Where death leaves us, there judgment finds us; and where judgment finds us, eternity will hold us fast forever and ever. Salvation delivers the soul from going down into the bottomless pit of hell. We, being justified, are no longer liable to punishment because we are no longer chargeable with guilt. Jesus Christ bore the wrath of God in His people's stead so that they might never bear it. He made a full atonement to the justice of God for the sins of all believers. Against those who believe, there remains no record of guilt; their transgressions are blotted out, for Christ Jesus has finished transgression, made an end of sin, and brought in everlasting righteousness.

What a comprehensive word *salvation* is! It is a triumphant deliverance from the guilt of sin, from the dominion of sin, from the curse of sin, from the punishment of sin, and ultimately from the very existence of sin. Salvation is the death of sin—its burial, its annihilation, and the very obliteration of its memory, for thus says the Lord, "Their sins and their lawless deeds I will remember no more" (Heb. 8:12). It is of these things that I write, and it is of these things that you must learn.

Dear reader, this is the weightiest subject I can bring to you. I pray that you will give earnest heed to this most pressing of all subjects as you read. Your own salvation is of the first importance, and for this reason I have at the outset set it before your mind's eye. But if you need one last incentive to think about your salvation, you may be helped to realize its value if you consider that God the Father thinks highly of salvation. It was on His mind before the earth ever was. He thinks salvation is a lofty business, for He gave His own Son so that He might save rebellious sinners.

And Jesus Christ, His one and only Son, His Well Beloved, thinks salvation most important, for He bled and died to accomplish it. Will anyone trivialize that which cost Him His life? If He came from heaven to earth, should we be slow to look from earth to heaven? Should that which cost the Savior a life of holy zeal and an agonizing death be a small matter with us? By the bloody sweat of Gethsemane, by the tortures of Gabbatha, and by the wounds of Golgotha, I beseech you, be assured that Christ's work of salvation is worthy of your highest and most anxious thoughts. It could not be that God the Father and God the Son should thus make a common sacrifice, the one giving His Son and the other giving Himself for salvation, and yet salvation should be a light and trivial thing.

And the Holy Spirit thinks it no trifle either, for He condescends to work continually in the new creation so that He may bring about salvation. He is often vexed and grieved, yet He continues His abiding labors that He may bring "many sons to glory" (Heb. 2:10). Do not despise what the Holy Spirit esteems lest you despise the Holy Spirit Himself. The sacred Trinity thinks much of your salvation, so do not neglect to think about your own salvation in Christ as well.

—Robert L. Reymond

CHAPTER 1

Effectual Calling

Whom He predestined, these He also called.
—ROMANS 8:30

Then Jesus entered and passed through Jericho. Now behold, there was a man named Zacchaeus who was a chief tax collector, and he was rich. And he sought to see who Jesus was.... And when Jesus came to the place, He looked up and saw him, and said to him, "Zacchaeus, make haste and come down, for today I must stay at your house." So he made haste and came down, and received Him joyfully....

Then Zacchaeus stood and said to the Lord, "Look, Lord, I give half of my goods to the poor; and if I have taken anything from anyone by false accusation, I restore fourfold."

And Jesus said to him, "Today salvation has come to this house, because he also is a son of Abraham."
—LUKE 19:1–3, 5–6, 8–9

It is always beneficial for Christians to receive instruction over and over again in the doctrines that lie at the base of our most holy religion, and among these critical matters is *effectual calling*. So after a thorough explanation of this important doctrine, I will use the case of Zacchaeus the tax man as a great illustration of God's effectual call of the sinner to Himself.

The divine Christ accomplished the salvation of the elect by His obedient life and sacrificial death at Calvary; by His doing and dying, He purchased and spread the banquet table of salvation. But how did we get in on it? Why are we at His banquet table? Even more personally, why did you and I trust Christ as our Savior when the unbeliever sitting in the pew next to us spurned Him? Were we simply smarter than our neighbor? No, that is not the reason. Isaac Watts's hymn captures how this has occurred:

> How sweet and awesome is the place
> With Christ within the doors,
> While everlasting love displays
> The choicest of her stores.
>
> While all our hearts and all our songs
> Join to admire the feast,
> Each of us cries, with thankful tongue,
> "Lord, why was I a guest?"
>
> "Why was I made to hear Your voice,
> And enter while there's room,
> When thousands make a wretched choice,
> And rather starve than come?"
>
> 'Twas the same love that spread the feast
> That sweetly drew us in;
> Else we had still refused to taste,
> And perished in our sin.

What Effectual Calling Means

The reason we are at the feast is that God effectually called us to Christ. So the application of our salvation, hard won by our Savior's accomplished atonement, begins with God the Father's irresistible summons by His word and Spirit to spiritually dead elect sinners such as we. This summons to enter into fellowship with Jesus Christ is normally issued in and by the public proclamation of the gospel. The Spirit of Christ, working by and with the Father's summons, regenerates spiritually dead elect sinners, enabling them thereby to repent of their sins and in faith to receive and to rest on Christ alone for their salvation. The moment people trust Christ, God justifies them, forgiving them of all their sins and declaring them righteous in His sight. He also definitively sanctifies them, adopts them into His family, and seals them to the day of redemption by the indwelling Spirit of adoption.

Sinners, now Christians, begin to experience the lifelong process of progressive, or processive, sanctification, by which they die more and more to sin and live more and more to righteousness, throughout which time they also persevere in holiness by the power of the Holy Spirit, with the end and goal of this entire series of divine acts and processes being their glorification, into which state they are finally brought in the eschaton at the return of Christ. At that point believers will be fully conformed to the image of the Son of God, and Christ will then be in the highest sense possible "the firstborn among many brethren" (Rom. 8:29). This entire application process begins with God's effectual call of the sinner into fellowship with Jesus Christ.

God's effectual calling, then, is the first drop of mercy in order of time that slakes the spiritual thirst of the condemned sinner. Carried out in accordance with God's eternal purpose (Rom. 8:28–29; 2 Tim. 1:9), it is heavenly in its origin (Heb. 3:1), holy in its character (2 Tim. 1:9), heavenward in its destination (Phil. 3:14), and irrevocable once it is issued (Rom. 11:29). By it God summons elect sinners (see 1 Cor. 1:26–30) into fellowship with Christ (1 Cor. 1:9), calls them "out of darkness into His marvelous light" (1 Peter 2:9), into His kingdom and to eternal glory (1 Thess. 2:12; 2 Thess. 2:14; 1 Peter 5:10), and finally to both the eschatological marriage supper of the Lamb (Rev. 19:9) and to eternal life (1 Tim. 6:12). By it the Christian is summoned to freedom from the law (Gal. 5:13), to one hope (Eph. 4:4), to a life of holiness as saints (1 Thess. 4:7; see Rom. 1:7; 1 Cor. 1:2), to following Christ by enduring suffering for well-doing (1 Peter 2:21; 3:9), and to peaceful human social relations (1 Cor. 7:15; Col. 3:15). In a sentence, effectually called sinners will begin to "walk worthy of the calling with which [they] were called" (Eph. 4:1).

In sum, Westminster Shorter Catechism (WSC), question 31, defines *effectual calling* as "the work of God's Spirit, whereby, convincing us of our sin and misery, enlightening our minds in the knowledge of Christ, and renewing our wills, he persuades and enables us to embrace Jesus Christ freely offered to us in the gospel." This, then, is what we mean by God's effectual calling of the sinner to salvation. The Victorian poet Francis Thompson captured this doctrine magnificently in his epic poem "The Hound of Heaven":

> I fled Him, down the nights and down the days;
> I fled Him, down the arches of the years;
> I fled Him, down the labyrinthine ways
> 　　Of my own mind; and in the mist of tears
> I hid from Him, and under running laughter.
> 　　Up vistaed hopes I sped;
> 　　And shot, precipitated,
> Adown titanic glooms of chasmèd fears,
> 　　From those strong Feet that followed, followed after.
> 　　　But with unhurrying chase,
> 　　　And unperturbéd pace,
> Deliberate speed, majestic instancy,
> 　　They beat—and a Voice beat
> 　　More instant than the Feet—
> "All things betray thee, who betrayest Me!"
>
> ───────────
>
> 　　Halts by me that footfall:
> 　　Is my gloom, after all,
> Shade of His hand, outstretched caressingly?
> 　　"Ah, fondest, blindest, weakest,
> 　　I am He Whom thou seekest!
> Thou dravest love from thee, who dravest Me."[1]

Such is Thompson's depiction of the Hound of Heaven's gracious effectual pursuit and capture of the elect sinner.

Zacchaeus, an Illustration of Effectual Calling

Having explained the doctrine, I will turn to the case of Zacchaeus, a glorious illustration of God's effectual calling. You probably know the story from Luke 19. As far as he understood, Zacchaeus, the chief

───────────

1. Francis Thompson, *The Hound of Heaven* (New York: Dodd, Mead and Co., 1925), 45, 60. "Dravest" means "drove."

tax collector of Jericho, simply had a curiosity to see the famous person Jesus of Nazareth, who was passing through town. Moved by this motive, the great crowds, and his short stature, Zacchaeus did as little boys are accustomed to do. He ran ahead and climbed up a sycamore-fig tree, where he could hide in the thick foliage to get a clear look at Jesus. But his curiosity to see Jesus was wrought in him by the Spirit of God, for no one takes a step toward Jesus in whose heart the Spirit of God has not already done His work.

At first, probably with some anxiety, Zacchaeus peered down from the tree branch on which he sat, wondering how he would recognize this man whom some people were saying was the Messiah. Jesus wore no pontifical garb; no beadle walked before Him carrying a silver mace as Rome prescribes must be done before the pope. How would Zacchaeus distinguish Him in that thronging crowd? He did not have to wonder long, for before he caught sight of Jesus, Jesus came, looked up, and, fixing His eyes on him, said, "Zacchaeus, make haste and come down, for today I must [*dei*] stay [literally "remain"] at your house." Down came Zacchaeus and received Him joyfully. Christ entered his home. Zacchaeus entered the kingdom of heaven and became Christ's follower. What a priceless picture, an exquisite depiction, of God's effectual call of the sinner into fellowship with His Son! There you have the doctrine superbly illustrated, but now I want to make some brief observations, using Zacchaeus's breathtaking salvation experience, to elaborate on God's effectual call of the sinner to salvation for your enjoyment, edification, and better understanding of "your own salvation" (Phil. 2:12) and how it occurs.

First, Zacchaeus's salvation that day makes clear that God's effectual call is *a gracious call*. We surmise this because Zacchaeus was the last character in Jericho we might conclude would be saved. He was an unscrupulous man, lost to Jewish society, to public respect, and to moral decency. We do not know anything about his parents, but very likely they were reputable people because they gave their son a name that means "righteous one" or "pure one," reflecting their fondest hopes for his future. Now they scarcely dared to whisper his name in polite society or in any company or even acknowledge that they knew him, for their son had joined the infamous trade of the tax collectors, not only becoming the head tax collector in Jericho but also becoming exceedingly rich by doing so. Scholars have noted of Zacchaeus,

> No doubt he was a sort of district tax commissioner who had purchased the Jericho tax franchise from the Roman or provincial government; he then probably farmed it out to subordinate tax agents who did the actual tax collecting, all of them reaping huge commissions and getting rich off poor and wealthy alike. Jericho was known for its palm groves and balsam (Josephus, *Antiquities*, 15.4.2) and was on the main load of traffic between major commercial centers west of the Jordan (Joppa, Jerusalem) and in the Transjordan. It was easy to amass a fortune there.[2]

While it was a galling and heavy grievance to the Jews that they had to pay tribute to a heathen power at all, they reserved their most intense hatred for any of their native countrymen who lent themselves to this obnoxious business. So for Jews, Zacchaeus was an outcast, a moral leper, the very offscouring of society. The Pharisees never looked at him; they passed him by as if he were a dog. And the ordinary people of Jericho cursed him under their breath. But God calls whom He wills, and He calls the worst of sinners from the worst of businesses. I have often thought it a great condescension on God's part even to look down on sinful people, but it was an equally great condescension on Jesus's part that day when He looked *up* to see this tax collector sitting in that tree. When God looks down on us, that is sheer mercy; and when Christ looked up at Zacchaeus, that was also sheer mercy indeed. Many people have climbed up in the tree of their alleged good works and have perched themselves among the branches of their alleged holy actions, trusting that by them they will be saved, but by no works other than Christ's will anyone be saved. Nevertheless, Christ graciously looks up even to such proud sinners and calls them down. "Come down," He says, "for today I must stay at your house." That is a gracious call of the most remarkable kind, would you not agree?

---

2. L. M. Petersen, "Zacchaeus," in *The Zondervan Encyclopedia of the Bible*, ed. Merrill C. Tenney and Moises Silva, 5 vols., rev. ed. (Grand Rapids: Zondervan, 2009), 5:1191, abbreviations expanded.

Second, Zacchaeus's salvation illustrates that God's effectual call is *a personal call*. There was no mistaking to whom our Lord's command was addressed. With divine omniscience He called this tax collector from Jericho to Himself by name. Here I must make a distinction: there is a general call addressed to all people by both the Spirit and the church when they say to sinners everywhere, "Come to Christ" (see Rev. 22:17), which all will finally reject unless the divine summons that is addressed to specific people, whom the Bible calls the elect, accompanies it. It is simply not correct to represent the church alone as the source of the external or outward invitation to salvation. After all, it is God's word that the church proclaims. In other words, it is God Himself, in the church's proclamation of His word, who outwardly summons all classes of people to repentance unto life and to faith in Jesus Christ (Isa. 45:22; 55:1; Matt. 11:28; Acts 17:30–31). When the church proclaims the gospel correctly, it will make it clear to its auditors that it is proclaiming the summons of God. But we must remember that the Bible teaches also that the race of humanity to whom God issues His general summons is spiritually dead (Eph. 2:1) and corrupt (Ps. 14:1–3); Romans 8:7 says that its collective mind "is not subject to the law of God" (that is its depravity), "nor indeed can [it] be" (that is its inability). It is only as God's effectual summons, quickening the dead sinner, accompanies His general summons that the elect sinner responds by repentance unto life and faith in Jesus Christ. God does not effectually call His people as a whole; He calls them personally, one by one. I could call all of you to faith throughout eternity, but if God does not call you who hear me one by one, my preaching will have no effect.

Third, Zacchaeus's salvation illustrates that God's effectual call is *a hastening call*. Jesus did not say, "Come down tomorrow"; He said, "Make haste and come down, for *today* I must stay at your house" (Luke 19:5). God does not call us to act tomorrow; the writer to the Hebrews says, "Today, if you will hear His voice, do not harden your hearts" (Heb. 3:15). Every tick of the clock says, "Now! Today!" Every beat of your pulse says, "Now! Today!" My heart says to you, "Now! Today!" The Holy Spirit says to you, "Now! Today!" *Tomorrow* is a day only in Satan's calendar. The Shakespearean character Macbeth soliloquizes,

> Tomorrow, and tomorrow, and tomorrow,
> Creeps in this petty pace from day to day
> To the last syllable of recorded time,
> And all our yesterdays have lighted fools
> The way to dusty death. Out, out, brief candle!
> Life's but a walking shadow, a poor player
> That struts and frets his hour upon the stage
> And then is heard no more: it is a tale
> Told by an idiot, full of sound and fury,
> Signifying nothing. (5.5.19–28)

Macbeth casts our passing days as only a sequence of words in the script of the play called time, "a tale told by an idiot, full of sound and fury, signifying nothing." But our days are far more, for they lead to eternal destinies, either to heaven or to hell. Tomorrow you may lift up your eyes in hell. Why then will you say, "I will come tomorrow"? You do not know that, for you do not know what a day, even the next minute, may bring forth.

Fourth, Zacchaeus's salvation illustrates that God's effectual call is *a humbling call.* It says to the sinner, "Come *down*, Zacchaeus." Many preachers, such as Robert Schuller with his *Self Esteem: The New Reformation*, call people to repentance in a fashion that makes them proud and exalts them in their own self-esteem. Such preachers tell them that God has done everything He can do to save them; now it is up to them. God has voted for them; the devil has voted against them; and now it is they who must exercise their free will and break the tie and cast the deciding vote. How democratic—placing God, the devil, and sinners all on a par as equals in effecting the sinner's salvation! But how heretical!

When people are told this, they are led to conclude that they can turn to God anytime they like, for it is they who decide when and where and even whether their salvation will occur. These ministers in doing so have in effect called them to go up in their own self-esteem, not to come down. But salvation is wholly the Lord's doing. The true gospel puts God first, God last, God in the middle, God throughout, God all and all, and God without end. The true gospel puts the crown wholly and solely on the head of Him who came to save people with no need of a helper. When God calls people, He calls them to come down—from the high branches of their self-sufficiency and from the bowers of their professed good works that are only filthy rags—to look no more to their self-improvement efforts; to come down until they see their corruption, their filthiness, and their wickedness. "Come down," says God when He effectually calls the sinner to salvation. "Come down and repent!" "I resist the proud," He says, "but I show grace to the humble" (see Prov. 3:34; James 4:6).

Fifth, Zacchaeus's salvation illustrates that God's effectual call is *an affectionate call*. "Today," Jesus said, "I must stay at your house" (Luke 19:5). You are not left to wonder what the people thought about that. They murmured and said, "He has gone to be a guest of a man who is a sinner." Perhaps a Jew was there who had been inside Zacchaeus's house; he might have been dragged there by one or more of Zacchaeus's agents and been impoverished by this man. Perhaps another Jew who had been inside Zacchaeus's house had been ordered to appear there and had been relieved of virtually all his property. They said, "What? This man is going into such a den of iniquity as that?"

Jesus's disciples also probably thought it a very imprudent thing to do. They did not say it, but I wonder if they did not think to themselves, "Master, forgive Zacchaeus if You must, but please do it privately. Accept him as a secret disciple, but do not publicly go into his house. It might injure Your character, and it will surely offend the people and certainly harm Your reputation."

But Jesus publicly said it was necessary for Him to go to Zacchaeus's house. Why did He do as He did? Because God's effectual call was an affectionate call. He did not say that He would stand at the edge of Zacchaeus's property or at the threshold of his door or look through a window. Jesus said it was needful that He reside for a time at Zacchaeus's house—the house where the tax collector had listened to widows' cries and orphans' weeping but had never been moved to compassion. "I will come there, Zacchaeus, where you, like a ravenous wolf, devoured your prey; I will come there and bless you with salvation." Oh, what affection there was in God's effectual summons to Zacchaeus!

Throughout Jesus's earthly ministry, it was the same. Those who showed contempt for Jesus's activities called Him derisively the friend of publicans and sinners (e.g., Matt. 11:19; Luke 7:34). Yes, Jesus did befriend sinners, even open sinners of the most undoubted degree of sin. Early in His ministry He spoke to the unchaste woman at the well of Sychar (John 4:1–26); then He refused to condemn the adulterous woman in John 8 but rather forgave her; and He finished His ministry by dispensing pardon to a thief on the cross (Luke 23:39–43). Throughout His ministry He was always receiving sinners and eating with them—that was the morals charge brought against Him.

This old contempt of the sinner's Savior and toward biblical Christianity lingers still among the self-righteous. Jesus and His religion are too lenient to the sinner, they say. His religion tends to discourage the virtuous and looks too favorably on the disreputable. It is always talking about pardon without the recipient of that pardon meriting it and always speaking slightingly of human goodness. It is a foe to decent society and an enemy of good morals. Those who talk this way have but a scanty supply of morals and virtues themselves, and when they speak this way, they simply show that they are standing in the line that populates hell.

Even within the evangelical church this proud attitude may lurk. Oh, we want to see people come to Christ, indeed, but privately we pray, "God, oh, let them be respectable sinners!" "Don't send us criminal types," we pray. "Don't send us homeless, impoverished people. Please, dear God, don't send us women of the street; don't send us smelly beggars. Please, dear God, send us middle- and upper-class sinners. We'll be more comfortable with them in our midst." How unlike this is our Savior, who was the friend of publicans and sinners, of thieves and adulterers! I would be delighted if God would send to His church some of His elect who are smelly beggars, for they might contribute to our humility and growth in grace by reminding us that we were, and in some respects still are, as foul and smelly as they before God cleaned us up. There is simply no room in the Christian church for snobbery.

Sixth, Zacchaeus's salvation illustrates that God's effectual call is *a staying call*. Jesus's call was not, "Today I will walk into your house through the front door and right out the back door." That is how the general call of the gospel affects a lot of people; it operates on them for a time, and then it is all over. Jesus did not say, "I am just dropping in to say hello, and then I will be on My way," but "I must *stay* at your house. I am coming to sit down and to eat and to drink with you. I must have a meal with you." Jesus does not come into your heart merely for a moment. He comes there to stay. "Oh," you say, "that is the kind of religion I want. I want a staying call, something that will last. I do not want a faith that will wash out; I want a colorfast faith." That is the kind of call and the kind of faith God and Jesus give. They say, "Today, I must stay at your house."

Seventh, Zacchaeus's salvation illustrates that God's effectual call is *a reassuring call.* Zacchaeus did not have to wonder whether he was saved; Christ gave him full assurance of his salvation, expressly declaring, "Today salvation has come to this house, because he also is a son of Abraham; for the Son of Man has come to seek and to save that which was lost" (Luke 19:9–10). So, I ask, are you trusting Christ? Then why do you fret and wonder whether you are saved or not? Christian, your Savior has told you that you are His, that you belong to Him, that He infallibly bought you with the price of His own blood. So stop wavering and start waving the palm branches of praise in full assurance that you belong to Him.

Eighth, Zacchaeus's salvation illustrates that God's call, as its name affirms, is *an effectual call.* It really works; it produces results. In Zacchaeus we see the fruits that God's effectual summons always produces. Zacchaeus's door was open, his table was spread, his heart was generous, his hands were washed, his mind was unburdened, his spirit was repentant, and his soul was joyful. Our loving Christ doubtless spoke words of life to Zacchaeus in his home, and he became a changed man. "Look, Lord," he said, "I give half of my goods to the poor; and if I have taken anything from anyone by false accusation, I restore fourfold" (Luke 19:8). Half his wealth was gone, along with another good portion of his money. Zacchaeus would go to bed that night a great deal poorer than when he climbed the tree in the morning, but a great deal richer, too—poorer in this world's goods but infinitely richer in heaven's treasures.

Christians, we know whether God has called us effectually by this: God's call produces good works as the lively fruit and evidence of saving faith. We do not believe that people have been genuinely converted unless they renounce the errors of their past life. If God has truly and effectually called a person to Christ, down the drain will go the store of strong liquor that is regularly intoxicating him, and up will go his praise to the Almighty for His grace in saving him. If God has truly and effectually called a person, all her shutters will go up on her business on the Lord's Day, and a sign will say, "This business is closed and will not be open again on the Lord's Day." If God has truly and effectually called a criminal who has robbed someone, he or she will restore whatever has been taken. If God has truly and effectually called you and tomorrow your favorite worldly amusement beckons, you will not go. Again, we do not believe that people have been genuinely converted unless, practically, Christ Himself becomes the Lord of their conscience and His law becomes their delight.

Ninth, Zacchaeus's salvation illustrates that Jesus's call is *a necessary call*. Jesus did not say to Zacchaeus, "I *might* stay at your house." The Greek is quite specific here. Jesus said, "Zacchaeus,... I *must* stay at your house" (Luke 19:5). It was necessary for Jesus to stay. An old saying is that "must is for kings"; kings say "must" to all their subjects and do not generally care to be told that they must do something. But here is the King, the likes of whom there never was or will be for glory and dominion, who is bound by a *must*. He said, "I *must* stay at your house." He said, "Other sheep I have which are not of this fold; them also I *must* bring" (John 10:16). He was under the mandate of His Father's effectual call.

The summons of sinners to faith in Christ is not a thing that God might do. He must do it. It is as much a necessity that He summon sinners to salvation as it is that He keep His covenant promise that never again will He drown the world in a flood. It is necessary for three reasons: because He eternally and immutably purposed to do so, because he eternally and immutably promised to do so, and because Christ infallibly purchased sinners at Calvary with the price of the blood of the eternal covenant. So when Christ tells the sinner that He must stay at his house, what can the poor sinner do but oblige Him?

When the Lord comes to this effectual *must*—that He must and will come into the sinner's life—it is all over with the sinner's resistance.

At other times a sinner can say, "I heard Him knocking. He knocked before, and He is knocking now. I put Him off before; I will put Him off again." But when the Lord declares, "Today, I must stay at your house," it is no longer left to sinners to deliberate whether they will let Him in or not. Whenever Jesus says, "I must," something will come of it. Who can resist His omnipotent *must*? Get out of the way, you demons; move aside, you wicked ones; flee, darkness; die, death! Difficulties vanish, and impossibilities are achieved. Crash goes the door, and in Jesus walks at the sinner's willing invitation. Grace is irresistible when it comes to God's effectual summons of His elect. God is Francis Thompson's "Hound of Heaven," and He will find and bring His prey to heel in His good time.

Tenth, in conclusion, I have one application to make about Zacchaeus's call to salvation. It is to *the despairing soul*. Perhaps an unscrupulous "Zacchaeus" is reading this book. Like him, you may be curious about Jesus and know that He is calling you, so come to Him, believe His love, trust His mercy. If you want to come, you may come, for it is Christ who summons you. Oh, that you might come to Him and be saved! Christ says, "Come down!" So humble yourself now in the sight of God. Confess your sins to Him; tell Him that you are a wretch and a worm. Then look to Him, for you may be assured that He first looked at you. You say, "I am willing to look, but I am afraid He is not willing to save me." If you are willing to look to Christ, He gave you that will. So believe on the Lord Jesus Christ, and He will save you. I trust that His Holy Spirit is calling you. Indeed, I trust that He is saying to you, "Make haste and come down, for today I must stay at your house," for if He is saying that to you, you will come, and you will be saved beyond a doubt.

Study Questions

1. What does *effectual calling* mean?

2. How is effectual calling illustrated in the poem "The Hound of Heaven"?

3. How does the account of Zacchaeus show that effectual calling is a gracious call?

4. What is the difference between the general gospel call and the personal, effectual call?

5. What does it mean that effectual calling is a "hastening" call?

6. How does the humbling call of God contradict the "self-esteem" gospel?

7. How did Christ's words to Zacchaeus show His affection for repentant sinners?

8. Why is it significant that the Lord Jesus chose to stay at Zacchaeus's house and not merely visit?

9. How do we see in Zacchaeus the effectual power of God's call to produce results?

10. Have you been effectually called by God? How do you know?

CHAPTER 2

Regeneration

I said to you, "You must be born again." The wind blows where it wishes, and you hear the sound of it, but cannot tell where it comes from and where it goes. So is everyone who is born of the Spirit.
—JOHN 3:7–8

In the first chapter I addressed the doctrine of effectual calling, whereby your personal salvation begins. The Westminster Shorter Catechism, question 31, defines *effectual calling* as "the work of God's Spirit, whereby convincing us of our sin and misery, enlightening our minds in the knowledge of Christ, and renewing our wills, he persuades and enables us to embrace Jesus Christ, freely offered to us in the gospel." The catechism does not have a question as such on regeneration but has embedded regeneration in its definition of effectual calling in such language as "enlightening our minds in the knowledge of Christ, and renewing our wills." So it is right and proper to follow effectual calling now with this chapter on regeneration, for it is the Holy Spirit's regenerating work that makes God's calling effectual.

The Miracle of Regeneration

We need not wonder that there are mysteries in our most holy faith, for there are mysteries everywhere. In nature there are millions of things that we cannot understand. If we go outside, we will, like Nicodemus, observe that the wind blows. We know it blows; we hear its sound and observe its effects. But as to where that wind came from before it reached us or where it goes after it passes us, we know little. Though we do not understand everything about the wind, yet we can make use of it. People have made use of the wind in hundreds of ways, yet it is not necessary that they understand everything in order to use it.

It is the same with our bodies; they are fearfully and wonderfully made, so there are inexplicable mysteries about them that leave the most learned scientists and physicians baffled. If we think for only a little while about even as simple a matter as how it is that food is gradually turned into flesh and health and physical strength, knowing how impossible it would be for us to do this by any chemical process or mechanical apparatus, we will acknowledge that there are mysteries in every physical life, secret chambers into which the full understanding of humanity cannot penetrate.

As there are mysteries all about us in even the most commonplace things of life, it should not be thought remarkable that there should be mysteries in the spiritual realm. Our Lord Jesus Christ, by using the metaphor of the wind when speaking of the regenerating work of the Holy Spirit, shows us clearly that it, too, is a mystery, but one that can be turned to practical account. A man may be an admirable sailor and yet know very little about the origin of wind. If he understands how to hoist, shift, and unfurl his sail, he will do well enough.

So it is with the mysteries of the kingdom of God. Although we cannot understand everything about God's kingdom, the practical use of some of the truths of it is a matter of such worth that we do well to learn as much as we can about them. I am not going to answer all the questions that may arise in your mind about God's work of regeneration. But I will make one point now that is altogether beyond dispute as far as the Bible is concerned: *If you are ever to be saved, you must experience the new birth—that is, the Spirit's regenerating work. Must* is for kings to declare, the saying goes, and it was the King of kings who said, "You must be born again," or "from above." This text belongs to the absolute necessities of the spiritual realm. Here is a truth that cannot be set aside. If you are ever to enter the kingdom of God or even to see it, if you are ever to be reconciled to the God whom you have greatly offended, "you must be born again." You must be regenerated. Said another way, a miracle wrought by God Himself must occur in your life if you would be saved.

John Blanchard, the British Reformed evangelist, relates the following story from his own ministry. He was invited to a church in Northern Ireland for a week of evangelistic preaching. When he got there, the pastor informed Blanchard that he was rather certain that every night two men would be sitting in the front pew. They would listen intently and then depart. They had done this for years, but they had never trusted Christ. Throughout the week, it was just as the pastor had said: here they were—these two men—and they seemed to hang on every word Blanchard spoke, then shake his hand and thank him and bid him good night. Toward the end of the week, Blanchard arranged to meet with them privately. They were very willing to talk with him. Blanchard explained the gospel to them, and both of them said they understood it. They said, "We know that all we need to do is to trust Christ to be saved, but we are not ready to do that yet. Someday we plan to do so, but not now."

Blanchard replied, "That is all you need to do, true enough, but that is not all you need."

With great surprise they asked, "What else do we need to do?"

Blanchard answered, "You misunderstand me. I did not say you needed to do something else. I said, 'Trusting Christ is what you need to do to be saved, but that is not all you need.'"

"What more do we need?" they asked.

Blanchard replied, "You need a miracle! You need the miracle of the Spirit's regenerating work in your hearts in order to repent of your sins and to believe in Christ. If the Spirit does not regenerate you, you will never believe and you will be eternally lost." The men were stunned to hear that, and both became very sober, saying they had thought that faith in Christ—the time, the place, the how—was all up to them.

"No," Blanchard said, "what you need to do is to cry out to God's Spirit to regenerate you, for if He does not do His work first, you will never be saved." They bowed their heads, asked God's Spirit to do His regenerating work within them, and that night they both trusted Christ as their Savior when Blanchard issued the gospel call.

The Meaning of Regeneration

Scripture has much to say about the gracious regenerating work of the Spirit. Paul employs the word *palingenesis*, translated "regeneration," only once in his writings with reference to the spiritual renewal of an individual: "Not by works of righteousness which we have done, but according to His mercy He saved us, through the washing of *regeneration* and renewing of the Holy Spirit" (Titus 3:5). Here we learn that regeneration washes us clean, clearly a metaphor for spiritual transformation. But Paul employs the doctrinal idea to which the word refers elsewhere in his writings under such terminology as, first, life-giving resurrection with Christ:

> God…gives life to the dead and calls those things which do not exist as though they did. (Rom. 4:17)

> When we were dead in trespasses, [He] made us alive together with Christ. (Eph. 2:5)

> You, being dead in your trespasses and the uncircumcision of your flesh, He has made alive together with Him. (Col. 2:13)

And second, as a divine work of creation:

> In Christ Jesus neither circumcision nor uncircumcision avails anything, but a new creation. (Gal. 6:15)

> If anyone is in Christ, he is a new creation. (2 Cor. 5:17)

> We are His workmanship, created in Christ Jesus. (Eph. 2:10)

And Peter writes that we are "born again," or God begets [us] anew (1 Peter 1:23), while James speaks of God bringing us forth (James 1:18). But it is particularly John, following the teaching of Jesus Himself, who is in a unique sense the theologian of the new birth, or birth from above. It is John who records Jesus's "Birth from Above" discourse with Nicodemus in John 3:1–15 and then refers eleven times in other places in his writings to God begetting.[1]

---

1. See John 1:13 ("who were born [begotten]…of God"); 1 John 2:29 ("is born of Him [has been begotten]"); 3:9 ("Whoever has been born [begotten] of God… has been born [begotten] of God"); 4:7 ("is born [begotten] of God"); 5:1 ("is born

By the divine act of regeneration, sinners are re-created in and to newness of life, have the defilement of their heart cleansed or washed away (Ezek. 36:25–26; John 3:5; Titus 3:5), and are enabled to "see" and to "enter" the kingdom of God by faith (John 3:3, 5). They are also enabled to repent and to believe in Jesus (John 1:12–13); to believe that Jesus is the Christ (1 John 5:1); to love others, particularly other Christians (1 John 4:7; 5:1); and to do righteousness and to shun the life of sin (1 John 3:9; 5:18).

Jesus expressly taught three times in John 6 that God alone by His Spirit working regenerates when He declared, "No one can come to Me unless the Father who sent Me draws him" (v. 44). How does the Father draw? By His Spirit's regenerating work. And, "Everyone who has heard and learned from the Father comes to Me" (v. 45). Why do those who have heard come? Because they have been regenerated by the Holy Spirit. And, "No one can come to Me unless it has been granted to him by My Father" (v. 65). Why does a person come to Christ? Because that person is dead in sin and needs new life from the Spirit. And as we have already observed from the analogy that Jesus drew between the physical wind's natural operation and the Spirit's regenerating work (John 3:8), in addition to both its facticity ("the wind blows") and its effects ("and you hear the sound of it"), Jesus also taught both its sovereignty ("the wind blows where it wishes") and its inscrutable mystery ("you…cannot tell where it comes from and where it goes"). And by His metaphor of a begetting from above to describe the Spirit's quickening work, Jesus underscored its divine monergism—that is, that God's Spirit alone regenerates. J. I. Packer observes:

> Infants do not induce, or cooperate in, their own procreation…; no more can those who are "dead in trespasses and sins" prompt the quickening operation of God's Spirit within them (see Eph. 2:1–10). Spiritual vivification is a free, and to man mysterious, exercise of divine power (John 3:8), not explicable in terms of the combination or cultivation of existing human resources (John 3:6), not caused or induced by any human efforts (John 1:12–13)

[begotten] of God…Him who begot…who is begotten of Him"); 5:4 ("whatever is born [begotten] of God"); and 5:18 ("whoever is born [begotten] of God…; He who has been born [begotten] of God").

or merits (Titus 3:3–7), and not, therefore, to be equated with, or attributed to, any of the experiences, decisions, and acts to which it gives rise and by which it may be known to have taken place.[2]

Jesus's metaphor points out how erroneous is the Arminian's construction of regeneration, which makes man's spiritual renewal dependent on the exercise of his free will and cooperation with grace; and liberalism's vision of regeneration, which denies the need for grace, prevenient or otherwise, altogether. These constructions are both wrong. In short, regeneration is the precondition of repentance unto life and faith in Jesus Christ and is in no way dependent on these for its appearance in the Christian life. Conversely, as we shall see, both repentance unto life and faith in Jesus Christ are dependent on the Spirit's regeneration, as effects are dependent on their cause. Regeneration must necessarily precede repentance and faith, and not the other way around.

Regeneration is not replacing the substance of fallen human nature with another substance, nor is it the change in one or more of the faculties of the fallen spiritual nature, nor is it the perfecting of the fallen spiritual nature. Rather, it is the subconscious implanting of the principle of totally new spiritual life in the soul. I cannot tell you everything about how the Holy Spirit operates on the unregenerate, but it is usually done in conjunction with the conscious reading or the public proclamation of the word. (John the Baptist's regeneration is an exception, for he was regenerated while still in his mother's womb [Luke 1:41].) As far as we know, the Holy Spirit works on the mind according to the laws of the mind by first illuminating elect sinners' understanding, enabling them thereby to respond in true repentance and true faith to the outward, or public, gospel proclamation directed to their conscious understanding and will. The Spirit's enabling regeneration exerts a marvelous power in the elect, producing such a wondrous effect that Scripture portrays regenerate people as new creations, much as if they had returned to their original nothingness and had been born anew in an altogether higher sphere.

---

2. J. I. Packer, "Regeneration," in *Evangelical Dictionary of Theology*, ed. Walter A. Elwell (Grand Rapids: Baker, 1984), 925.

Creation is necessarily a work that happens in an instant, for a thing either is or it is not. There is no intervening space between non-existence and existence. Immediacy is God's method of creating. All through the primal creation week, God spoke, and it came to pass; He commanded, and it stood fast. So in His new creation work, there was a second when grace was not present in the soul, and in the next second it was. We may logically assume that a marked boundary line exists between those two seconds. But we do not have to rely here on logic alone. We have what Holy Scripture teaches.

Think for a moment about our Lord's miracles as an analogy. He turned water immediately into wine (John 2:1–11). He cursed the fig tree, and immediately it withered (Matt. 21:18–22; Mark 11:12–14). He immediately multiplied the loaves and fishes (Matt. 14:13–21; Mark 6:30–44; Luke 9:10–17; John 6:1–15). He said to the paralytic on his bed, "Rise, take up your bed and walk," and immediately he did so (John 5:8). He cured the leper immediately with a touch (Matt. 8:1–4; Mark 1:40–45; Luke 5:12–14); demons immediately fled from their captives at His command (e.g., Mark 5:1–20); deaf ears were opened (Mark 7:31–37); and withered limbs were restored instantly (Matt. 12:9–14; Mark 3:1–6; Luke 6:6–11). He said to the little dead girl, "Talitha, cumi" ("Little girl, I say to you, arise"), and she opened her eyes (Mark 5:41–42). He said to the dead son of the widow of Nain, "Young man, I say to you, arise," and he did so (Luke 7:14). He commanded the already corrupting Lazarus to come forth, and out of the tomb he came (John 11:43–44).

Just as Jesus exercised His power over people's bodies, so also the Holy Spirit does the same with people's souls. His regenerating work effects an instantaneous change in people that begins at once to govern their intellect and moral judgment, influences their will, and gives them new affections. Their new nature hates what their old nature that is destined to die loves, and it loves what their old nature hates. Their new nature is akin to and after the likeness of the nature of God Himself. Examples of this instantaneous work of regeneration abound in Scripture. Matthew is sitting at the receipt of custom; Jesus says to him, "Follow Me," and he rises and follows Jesus (Matt. 9:9). The Samaritan woman comes to the city well to draw water; Jesus speaks to her, and she goes away to tell the men of the city what Jesus has done for her (John 4:1–26). Zacchaeus is in a tree, and Jesus commands him to come down; he does so and, as a regenerated man, receives Jesus into his house (Luke 19:1–9). Jesus teaches that the tax collector who prays the simple prayer, "O God, look on me, the sinner, through the blood of the mercy seat," went down to his house having been justified (see Luke 18:13–14).

Peter preaches to the multitudes on the day of Pentecost. Three thousand people are pricked in their hearts, and they ask, "What shall we do?" That day they are saved and baptized (Acts 2:14–41). Jesus confronts Saul, who was breathing out threats and murder against the church, on the Damascus road and immediately converts him (9:1–9). Lydia is listening to Paul, and the Lord opens her heart to respond to the things spoken by the apostle (16:14). The Philippian jailer is in bed. There is an earthquake, and thinking that his prisoners have all escaped, he cries to Paul, who reassures him that all the prisoners are there. Rushing in, he falls at Paul's feet and asks, "What must I do to be saved?" He believes in Jesus then and there and is baptized that very night (16:25–34). It would be much more difficult, if not impossible, to find a gradual regeneration in Scripture than a sudden one, for here they are—men and women streaming to Jesus who are immediately transformed because of the regenerating work of the Spirit of God. No words have captured better both the divine monergism and the inevitable immediate effects of the Spirit's regenerating work than the following stanza from Charles Wesley's great hymn "And Can It Be That I Should Gain":

> Long my imprisoned spirit lay
> Fast bound in sin and nature's night;
> Thine eye diffused a quick'ning ray,
> I woke, the dungeon flamed with light;
> My chains fell off, my heart was free;
> I rose, went forth, and followed Thee.

The Holy Spirit's Regenerating Work

Regeneration will have its precursors. The gospel will be preached and heard, arguments will be made for the truthfulness of the Christian faith, and people may be induced thereby to give a studied hearing to them. But such things are not regeneration; they are the precursors of regeneration. For when regeneration occurs, regenerate people, having been commanded to repent and to believe, will immediately repent of their sin and place their trust in Jesus Christ.

We can illustrate this doctrine in many ways, but one of the best biblical descriptions of the Spirit's regenerating work is found in Ephesians 2:1–6, where Paul tells us that we

> were dead in trespasses and sins, in which [we] once walked according to the course of this world, according to the prince of the power of the air, the spirit who now works in the sons of disobedience, among whom also we all once conducted ourselves in the lusts of our flesh, fulfilling the desires of the flesh and of the mind, and were by nature children of wrath....
>
> *But God*, who is rich in mercy, because of His great love with which He loved us, even when we were dead in trespasses, *made us alive*...with Christ...and raised us up...and made us sit...in the heavenly places in Christ Jesus.

We *were* dead, says Paul; we *were* by nature children of wrath. Now we *are* alive, children of God. And between these two states, as the sole explanation for this transformation, stands the great act of regeneration. The God who is rich in mercy came to us and quickened us, regenerated us, made us alive by His Spirit. Can there be a greater miracle than that? That is why believers are trophies of grace. Let's look more closely at this passage.

What We Were Before

We were by nature people at whom God could look only with wrath. "By nature" means that we were born so. The way that modern culture extols the excellence of human nature is all idle talk. "The heart is deceitful above all things, and desperately wicked," wrote Jeremiah (Jer. 17:9). "Out of the heart proceed evil thoughts, murders, adulteries, fornications, thefts, false witness, blasphemies," taught Jesus in Matthew 15:19. Everything that is evil lurks in our hearts. And the very best of us, before we were regenerated, under the proper provocation could have committed the foulest sin. At that time, we were utterly insensible to spiritual things. The things of the Spirit were foolishness to us, and we would not receive them.

We may have heard the law of God preached and may have been pleased with the preacher's oratory and may have been moved by his earnestness, but we were never led by all of his pleadings to hate sin. We were shaken, but we were not awakened; we were insensible, spiritually, to the power of the law. We heard it and for a brief time may have been somewhat disquieted, but we never felt the terror of the condemnation that God pronounces on the sinner who breaks His law. We saw our face in the mirror of the law, but we did not wash, and sin's spots remained. If we did anything, it was to get away from the law's influence and drown all thoughts of the wrath of God in our old pleasures and sins. And we may have heard the gospel proclaimed as well, but its sweet notes were not music to our ears. What did we care for Jesus and His bleeding wounds? What respect did we have for His infinite love and the invitations of His precious word? We came and we went, but we continued as we were and never loved Jesus.

Some of us had grown so insensitive to spiritual things that we did not want to hear the gospel, so we stopped attending church. The Lord's Day became just like any other day of the week for us, except that we found most of our pleasures then. We went further in sin than we ordinarily did, for our daily labors kept us pretty steady during the week. The Lord's Day became for us the door of sin rather than the gate of mercy. We saw others going to church on Sunday morning and in the evening, but we were in our shirtsleeves working in our yard or in our casual clothes all day, and we said, "I do not care to go to listen to that dry talk. What nonsense!"

We did not desire the water of life or even believe in its existence. We had no interest in the doctrines of grace, and we certainly did not want or feel the need for the grace of the Lord Jesus Christ. He who is the Bread of Life held, at best, only a passing interest for us. We thought we were strong sand could find our own way to heaven. We believed that we were fat and flourishing, and therefore we did not want to feed on Him. No matter how the minister of God tried to charm us, we deaf adders would not be charmed. The movement of godly desire, of a humble hope, or of a holy wish was not in our souls.

We did not pray or ask God for anything. If we did pray, we might as well have mumbled our prayers backward as forward for any good there was in them. We prayed dead prayers, for there was no life in us. We just repeated the same prayers that we had learned as children. One man was so entrenched in his childhood prayers that, at the age of seventy, he still prayed that God would bless his father and mother who had been dead for thirty years! And while most of us thought that we were quite respectable, many of us became familiar with the pleasures of this world—its vanities, its gaieties, and its pollutions—and were not ashamed in the slightest. Indeed, we complimented ourselves that we were not as bad as others. Yet we did not want our secret deeds paraded before others. And why all this? All because we were dead, spiritually insensitive; we were by nature children of wrath.

What We Are Now
We are now alive and God's adopted children, heirs of God and joint heirs with Jesus Christ. We have passed from death to life. Now we sorrow for our treason against the infinite love of God. Now we love Jesus supremely. We gladly take up our cross and would willingly die for Him. We consciously know that a change, altogether supernatural, has taken place in us, because such a change would never have occurred had God left us to ourselves. We have passed from darkness to light, from the power of sin and Satan to God. We are as different from what we were as though we had died and risen from the dead. We are so different from what we used to be that if we met our old selves now we would not know ourselves.

We who are Christians despise what we once thought were our beauty and our comeliness; now we find our beauty in Christ, the all lovely one. We also have passed from fear to faith, from unhappiness to overflowing joy that is unspeakable and full of glory. Old things have passed away; for us everything now is new. We know that there is no condemnation for us who have believed in Jesus and that nothing can be laid to our charge, for all our sins have been placed on our glorious Savior. We know that Christ has made full atonement, and His work is the bliss of our lives. The things that once made us glad, if we were to do them now, would make us very sad; and the things that we thought would bring only melancholy then are now our highest joy. We no longer merely talk about God; we know Him and love Him. His promises are our riches. And the people of God who once we shunned as common and not very intelligent we now love for Christ's sake even as the world hates them. We enjoy being with them; we sing, pray, and worship with them. We now have an appetite for spiritual things that only Jesus can satisfy. We love the house of God. We love the Bible; the preaching ordinance of God's house blesses us, and we are filled by it as with marrow and fatness. And whereas before our fate was eternal death, now we have eternal life that can never be taken away from us.

How This Transformation Occurred
This transformation occurred because God, by His blessed Spirit, working by and with the word of God in our hearts, quickened us and made us alive in Christ Jesus. We can speak of the outward means and the external circumstances that preceded and accompanied it, but we can never capture with words the sacred way of the Spirit's dealings with us in regeneration.

Just make sure that you have received the miracle of divine quickening that I have been describing. Make sure that the "but God" of Ephesians 2:4 is in your life. These two words summarize the specific message that the Christian faith alone has to offer mankind. In their context, these two words contain the whole of the gospel. The gospel tells us of what God has done. It tells us about something that comes entirely from outside us and displays to us that amazing, astonishing, and gracious work of God that the apostle describes and defines in terms of quickening. I would ask you to search your heart and to ask yourself: "Do I have this 'but God' in my life?" Has God come in His grace and power and regenerated you by His Spirit so that you have this new outlook on life? If you do, thank God forever that it is so.

Study Questions

1. Why is regeneration called a miracle?

2. What does *regeneration* mean?

3. How do the Scriptures show that regeneration does not depend on man's free will?

4. How does the Holy Spirit ordinarily use God's word in regeneration?

5. How is regeneration like God's work of creating the world?

6. What evidence is there in the Bible that regeneration takes place in an instant?

7. How does the hymn "And Can It Be That I Should Gain?" illustrate regeneration?

8. What was our state before the Holy Spirit's regenerating work?

9. What is the state of believers after regeneration?

10. How should the doctrine of regeneration both humble believers and fill them with gratitude toward God?

CHAPTER 3

Repentance unto Life

Jesus came…preaching the gospel of the kingdom of God, and saying, "The time is fulfilled, and the kingdom of God is at hand. Repent, and believe in the gospel."

—MARK 1:14–15

I kept back nothing that was helpful, but proclaimed it to you, and taught you publicly and from house to house, testifying to Jews, and also to Greeks, repentance toward God and faith toward our Lord Jesus Christ.

—ACTS 20:20–21

We have seen that the application of the benefits of Christ's atoning work begins with God's effectual calling, which is made effectual through the Holy Spirit's regenerating work. These two benefits—God's effectual calling by the Spirit's regeneration—are God's works entirely. But when we move on in the biblical order of application, we discover that the sinner's response to the Father's summons and to the Holy Spirit's regenerating work is both repentance unto life and faith in Jesus Christ, both of which we do, but only by the grace of God, for as we will see, both are gifts of God. These two responses are twins, and to say which is the older brother is beyond our knowledge because they come into the soul together. This much is clear: though they differ in several respects, repentance is perfectly consistent with faith, and faith is perfectly consistent with repentance. Mark 1:15 tells us that Jesus began His ministry by preaching both: "The time is fulfilled, and the kingdom of God is at hand," He said. "Repent, and believe in the gospel." But because Jesus and Paul put repentance first, we will follow their lead and treat repentance first.

The Necessity of Repentance

Because the wise framers of the Westminster Confession of Faith (WCF) understood the human desire to be accepted by others, they realized that the minister of the gospel might be tempted to proclaim faith in Jesus Christ as the sole necessary response to the gospel proclamation to the neglect of preaching repentance as equally necessary for salvation. They understood that when and where this is done, the faith in Jesus Christ that the minister then elicits from sinners is abstracted from their need for salvation from sin, the only context that gives faith in Jesus Christ its significance. Such faith, absent the clarion call to repent and the resulting response of repentance, they also understood, inevitably takes on the dimensions of "easy decisionism" for the respondent, which is no true faith at all. Therefore, even before they define the doctrine of repentance, they remind the minister that preaching repentance is not to be regarded as a foreign or disrupting element in gospel proclamation. To the contrary, they describe it as an aspect of evangelical preaching. And they insist that none may hope for pardon without repentance, even though it is not to be rested in as if it were itself a satisfaction for sin or the cause of pardon, for repentance per se is and can be neither. In this connection do we not sing,

> Could my zeal no respite know,
> Could my tears forever flow,
> All for sin could not atone;
> Thou must save, and Thou alone.[1]

And,

> Not what I feel or do
> Can give me peace with God,
> Not all my prayers and sighs and tears
> Can bear my awful load.[2]

---

1. Augustus Toplady, "Rock of Ages, Cleft for Me," in the public domain.
2. Horatius Bonar, "Not What My Hands Have Done," in the public domain.

What, then, is the biblical ground for the confession's insistence that the minister of the gospel must proclaim repentance unto life along with his summons to faith in Jesus Christ? The Old Testament employs two verbs meaning "turn," "return," and "repent" when it calls for or speaks of repentance:

> Let the wicked forsake his way,
> And the unrighteous man his thoughts;
> Let him *return* to the LORD,
> And He will have mercy on him;
> And to our God,
> For He will abundantly pardon. (Isa. 55:7)

> "Now, therefore," says the LORD,
> *Turn* to Me with all your heart,
> With fasting, with weeping, and with mourning."
> So rend your heart, and not your garments;
> *Return* to the LORD your God,
> For He is gracious and merciful,
> Slow to anger, and of great kindness,
> And He relents from doing harm. (Joel 2:12–13)

> "As I live," says the Lord GOD, "I have no pleasure in the death of the wicked, but that the wicked *turn* from his way and live. Turn, turn from your evil ways! For why should you die, O house of Israel?" (Ezek. 33:11)

> I listened and heard,
> But they do not speak aright.
> No man *repented* of his wickedness,
> Saying, "What have I done?" (Jer. 8:6)

The word groups denoting *repentance* in the New Testament primarily mean "to change one's mind" and, secondarily, "to turn" and "to turn about," respectively. As did John the Baptist before Him (Matt. 3:2, 8, 11; Mark 1:4; Luke 3:3, 8; Acts 13:24; 19:4), Jesus preached repentance (Matt. 4:17; Mark 1:15), and He characterized His purpose in coming to people in terms of calling sinners to repentance (Luke 5:32). He warned that unless sinners repented, they would perish (Luke 13:3, 5) and that unless they were converted and became as little children, they would never enter the kingdom of heaven (Matt. 18:3). He denounced whole cities that would not repent, while commending Nineveh for repenting at the preaching of Jonah (Matt. 11:20–21; 12:41; Luke 10:13; 11:32). And He declared that heaven rejoices over one sinner who repents (Luke 15:7, 10). The glorified Christ taught beyond all doubt that repentance is to be a part of the church's gospel proclamation when He declared on the evening of His resurrection from the dead, "Thus it is written, and thus it was necessary for the Christ to suffer and to rise from the dead the third day, and that repentance and remission of sins should be preached in His name to all nations" (Luke 24:46–47). On their preaching missions throughout Galilee, the apostles "preached that people should repent" (Mark 6:12), and they continued to be true to this aspect of their Lord's commission throughout the book of Acts.[3] The author of Hebrews indicates that "repentance from dead works" (6:1) is a first principle of the doctrine of Christ. So as a minister of God, I must preach repentance.

Repentance Is a Gift of God

Another point is this: as the response to God's sovereign, effectual summons that was procured by Christ's cross work (as is every spiritual blessing the Christian receives) and made effectual by His Spirit's regenerating operations in the soul, repentance unto life is uniformly represented in Scripture as a gift of God. The psalmist prayed, "Restore us, O God…and we shall be saved" (Ps. 80:3; see also vv. 7, 19); Ephraim prayed, "Restore me, and I will return" (Jer. 31:18); and Jeremiah prayed, "Turn us back to You, O LORD, and we will be restored" (Lam. 5:21). Peter declared that God exalted Christ to His own right hand as Prince and Savior "to *give* repentance to Israel and forgiveness of sins" (Acts 5:31). On hearing Peter's testimony regarding the conversion of Cornelius's household, the Jerusalem church "glorified God, saying, 'Then God has also *granted* to the Gentiles repentance to life'" (Acts 11:18). And Paul instructed Timothy that the Lord's servant should gently correct the non-Christian opposition about him "if God

---

3. In the case of Peter, see Acts 2:38; 3:19; 8:22. In the case of Paul, see Acts 17:30; 20:21; 26:20.

perhaps will *grant* them repentance, so that they may know the truth" (2 Tim. 2:25).

Godly Sorrow versus Worldly Sorrow

We must understand that there is a distinction between godly sorrow for sin and mere worldly sorrow. Godly sorrow for sin that leads to true repentance is characterized in Acts 11:18 as "repentance to life." In 2 Corinthians 7:10 it is described as "repentance leading to salvation, not to be regretted." In 2 Timothy 2:25 Paul writes of a "repentance, so that they may know the truth," which must be distinguished from what he calls in 2 Corinthians 7:10 "the sorrow of the world [that] produces death." Here is the reason the catechism speaks not just of repentance but of repentance *unto life*.

Paul's "sorrow of the world [that] produces death" is amply illustrated by the rich young ruler and by Judas. When he heard Jesus's requirements for discipleship, the rich young ruler "became very sorrowful" (Luke 18:23). But his was a worldly sorrow because, being "very rich," he regarded his wealth as of greater value than the privilege of following Jesus, so he went away. And when Judas, seeing that Jesus had been condemned, "was remorseful and brought back the thirty pieces of silver" (Matt. 27:3). But his was a worldly remorse because it did not lead to the repentance that leaves no regrets and leads to salvation. Instead, it drove him to suicide. But to the Corinthians Paul writes in 2 Corinthians 7:9–11,

> Now I rejoice, not that you were made sorry, but that your sorrow led to repentance. For you were made sorry in a godly manner.… For godly sorrow produces repentance leading to salvation, not to be regretted; but the sorrow of the world produces death. For observe this very thing, that you sorrowed in a godly manner: What diligence it produced in you, what clearing of yourselves, what indignation, what fear, what vehement desire, what zeal, what vindication! In all things you proved yourselves to be clear in this matter.

Scripture is quite clear that people may feel remorse over their sins for any number of reasons. Often they are sorrowful only because they were apprehended. But unless their sorrow for sin is their response to the sight and sense not only of the danger but also of the filthiness and odiousness of their sins as contrary to the holy nature and righteous law of God, which then compels them so to grieve for and to hate their sins that they turn from them to God with full purpose and endeavor to walk with Him in all the ways of His commandments, it must be judged as merely "the sorrow of the world [that] produces death." Godly sorrow, the sinner's response to the Spirit's regenerating work in the soul, which normally accompanies the evangelical preaching of the doctrine of repentance, produces "repentance leading to salvation, not to be regretted."

In summary, the Westminster Shorter Catechism, question 87, defines what it carefully calls *repentance unto life* as "a saving grace, whereby a sinner out of a true sense of his sin, and apprehension of the mercy of God in Christ, doth, with grief and hatred of his sin, turn from it unto God, with full purpose of, and endeavor after, new obedience."

Repentance entails a radical and conscious change of view (a transformed intellect), a radical and conscious change of feeling (transformed emotions), and a radical and conscious change of purpose (a transformed volition) with respect to God, ourselves, sin, and righteousness. We acknowledge that we are sinners and that our sin entails personal guilt, defilement, and helplessness before God; we sorrow with a godly sorrow for the sins we have committed against the holy and just God; and we resolve to seek pardon and cleansing from God through the blood of Christ that alone satisfies the offended justice of God. So in turning from our sins in repentance, we turn to Christ in faith for salvation. Conversely, in turning to Christ in faith for salvation, we turn from our sins in repentance. God does not want us to preach repentance as a trifle, and the change of mind of which repentance speaks is a very deep and solemn work. There must be sorrow for sin and hatred of it in true repentance. I think there is no better definition of *repentance* than that of the children's hymn "Since Jesus Christ Was Sent to Save Us":

> Repentance is to leave
> The sins we loved before,
> And show that we in earnest grieve,
> By doing so no more.

False Repentance

As I have said, true repentance is consistent with true faith, and knowing this helps us to understand repentance better. I will explain.

First, we may be sure that unbelief is behind an understanding of repentance for people who conclude that their sin is too great for Christ to pardon. To believe this, even sincerely, is not truly to repent. Even people who are truly repentant can be tempted to believe that their sins are too great for Christ to pardon. To believe that is sinful in itself. It is a grievous sin, for it undervalues the merit of Christ's blood. It is a denial of the truthfulness of God's promise and detracts from the grace and favor of God, who sent His Son to save sinners. If you have such a persuasion, you must ask God to rid you of it, for it came from Satan and not from the Holy Spirit. God the Holy Spirit will never teach people that their sins are too great or too many to be forgiven. And if you are troubled because you have never been haunted by this belief, be glad instead of troubled. For we may all be assured that Christ can save anybody, and it is a wicked falsehood and a high insult against the majesty of divine love when people are tempted to believe that they are past the mercy of God. To believe that about yourself is not repentance unto life but worldly sorrow that produces death. It is a foul sin against the infinite mercy of God.

There is a second kind of spurious repentance that makes people dwell on the consequences of sin rather than on sin itself, and this keeps them from trusting Christ. Some people are so tormented and so distressed with fears of hell and thoughts of eternal judgment that they do not want to think about their future. So they go no further; they do not turn to Christ. This too is not true repentance. These torments may accompany true repentance but are not essential to it. That which the Puritans called *law work*, in which sinners are terrified with the horrible thought that God's mercy has passed them by forever, God may permit for some special purpose, but it is not true repentance, for any repentance that keeps a person from believing in Christ is a repentance that needs to be repented of. Any repentance that makes a person think Christ cannot or will not save him or her goes beyond and against the truth, and the sooner the one who believes this false notion is rid of it the better, for the repentance that leads to life and salvation is quite consistent with faith in Christ.

There is a third false repentance that leads people to hardness of heart and to despair. Some people are so seared with burning remorse as with a hot iron that they say, "We have done much evil, and there is no hope for us; therefore, we will not listen to the word of God anymore." And should they hear it, their hearts are as hard as stone. If they could once get the thought that God would forgive them, their hearts would flow with rivers of gratitude. But they feel a kind of regret that they have done wrong and go on in the same way they always have because they feel that there is no hope for them. They think that they may as well continue to live as they are accustomed to and enjoy the pleasures of sin, at least for a season, since they cannot ever enjoy the pleasures of grace. This also is not true repentance. It is a fire from hell that has hardened the spirit, and if you have never been the subject of such remorse, do not desire it. Do not long for needless terrors.

Jesus saves not by what you feel but by what you believe about His finished work, the blood and righteousness that God accepted on behalf of His people. Always remember that no repentance is worth having that is inconsistent with faith in Christ or that keeps one from believing in Christ. Any so-called repentance, even if it sinks a person as low as hell, is of no use except it is accompanied by a faith that lifts him or her up to heaven. People may loathe and detest themselves and all the while believe that Christ is able to save and has saved them. This is how true Christians live. They repent as bitterly for sin as if they knew they were going to be damned for it, but they rejoice as much in Christ as if their sin were nothing at all.

True Repentance

Having shown you what true repentance is not, I will focus now on what true repentance is. True repentance strips of all pride and is always accompanied by true faith in Christ that clothes with humility. True repentance ejects sin as an evil tenant and is always accompanied by true faith that admits Christ as the rightful Master of the house. True repentance purges the soul from dead works and is always accompanied by true faith that fills the soul with living works. True repentance ordains that there be a time for weeping and is always accompanied by true faith that announces there is a time for dancing. True repentance makes sinners weep and abhor their past life and is always accompanied by true faith in Christ that elates them because He has pardoned them. True repentance looks at the mountainous pile of sins that made Christ's death necessary and is always accompanied by true faith that looks at the sorrow of Jesus and His bleeding wounds and knows that He was nailed to the cross for those sins. True repentance leads believers to resolve that in the future they will not live as they have in the past, according to the lusts of the flesh, and is always accompanied by true faith that leads them to resolve to live like Jesus, who redeemed not with corruptible things, like silver and gold, but with His own precious blood. This is the repentance that leads to life and salvation. These two things, repentance and faith—always together—make up the work of grace in the soul whereby people are saved.

The Reasonableness of God

Is it unreasonable that God should demand that sinners repent? Here is a person who has offended you. You are ready to forgive him. Do you think it is overbearing or too exacting on your part if you ask him for an apology, acknowledging that he has wronged you, even as you forgive him? No, you do not. So also God, our sovereign monarch, against whom we have rebelled, sees it as inconsistent with the dignity of His kingship to absolve an offender who expresses no contrition. I ask again, Is God harsh, unreasonable, too demanding when He commands the sinner to repent? Does He not ask of you that which your own heart, if it were in a right state, would be only too willing to give?

Also, why should God allow you to love your sins and yet enter into His heaven? Your love of sin would make His heaven hell. Think for a moment: Can poison be in your veins, and you still be healthy? Can you harbor disease in your body and still be in good health? It is absurd to think so. Just so, repentance is founded on the necessity of moral rightness. It is your reasonable service. Oh, that people were reasonable! If they were, they would repent. It is because they are not reasonable that the Holy Spirit must teach them right reason before they will repent.

A Divine Command That Demands Obedience

I cannot allow you to think that there is no great alarm, that there is no reason why you should not think about your soul now. Many of us have seen and heard the sights and sounds of a great military review, with its stirring drums and martial music, its crack of rifles, and on occasion, even the thundering boom of a cannon. But suppose what you were seeing or hearing were a real war just a block away from your house; you would not sit so comfortably in your family room listening to all the noises of war.

I tell you that your sin is terrible and that Christ is the only Savior from sin. What do you think of these things? If you yawn and shrug your shoulders, you show that you do not think this is true. If you have not repented but can sit quite comfortably, you do not think that your sin is monstrously real. You do not really think that the God who made you demands that you should repent. But your sin *is* real, and God's command to repent *is* real. It is your procrastination and your self-confidence that are a sham, the bubble that will soon burst. God's command to repent is a solemn reality, and if you could but really and truly hear it as it should be heard, you would turn and flee for refuge to the only hope that is set before you in the gospel, and you would do it today. Today is God's time for repentance! "Today, if you will hear His voice, do not harden your hearts as in the rebellion" (Heb. 3:15).

"Today," the gospel always cries, for if it tolerated a single sin a single second it would be an unholy gospel. If the Bible told you to repent tomorrow, it would be allowing you to continue in sin today, and that would pander to human lusts, which God will never do. But the Bible makes a clean sweep of sin, and it demands that people throw down their weapons of rebellion now and repent of their sins today. So down with your weaponry! You must not keep one of them! Throw them down at once. As long as you continue unrepentant you continue in your sin and are increasing your sin by your refusal to repent. Today is your time to repent. It is the only time you can call your own. Tomorrow! Is there such a thing? In what calendar is it written except in the almanac of the fool? Tomorrow! O how that word "tomorrow" has ruined the lives of multitudes! "I will repent tomorrow," men say. But they are like the rear wheels of a car that are always near the front wheels but never get one inch nearer no matter how far or fast they go. "Tomorrow" is still beyond them, yes, only a day, but they never come to Christ. They speak as the old poet who said:

> I will tomorrow, that I will, I will be sure to do it.
> Tomorrow comes, tomorrow goes, and still I have "to do it."
> Thus, then, repentance is deferred from one day to another,
> until the day of death is one, and judgment is the other.

It is impossible for you now to repent unless the Spirit of God is with you. What makes you think, then, it will be more likely tomorrow that you will repent? But if you repent, the Spirit of God is in it, and when I command you, "Repent," He who bade me command you to do so gives power with the command, even as Christ commanded the waves to be still and they were quiet. So should your proud heart yield, it is because of the grace that accompanies the command. May it be so even now for any who need to repent. May God make you willing in this day of His power.

Finally, while God's command to repent has immediate power, it also has continual force. "Repent" is advice not only for the reckless youngster who needs Christ; it is advice also for the elderly Christian, for this is what we must do all our life long. The eleventh-century theologian Anselm said, "The sinner that I am, I have spent all my life repenting of my whole life." When he was nearing death in 1833, British preacher Rowland Hill said he had one regret, and that was that a "dear friend" who had lived with him for sixty years would have to leave him at the gate of heaven. And that "dear friend," he said, was repentance. "Repentance has been with me almost all my life, and I think that I shall shed a tear as I go through the gate to think that I cannot repent more than I did."

Repentance is the daily, hourly duty of the Christian. Christians should repent after they are saved more than they ever did before they were saved, for now they are far more aware of their sins. Christians will take themselves to task because only the thought of evil flits through their mind. And were it not that they still continue to look every moment to Christ, one foul imagination would cause them such a plague of pain that they would have no peace or rest. And when temptation comes, Christians find use of repentance, for, having hated sin and fled from it, they know that they have ceased to be what they once were. The more Christians know of Christ's love, the more they will hate themselves to think that they have sinned against such love. Indeed, every doctrine of grace will make a Christian repent. "How could I have ever sinned," he says, "I who was one of God's favored ones, chosen from before the creation of the world?" "How can I ever sin again," she says, "knowing that I am loved so much and kept so surely?" "How can I be so villainous as to sin against everlasting mercy?" Take any doctrine of grace you please, and Christians will make it not only a reason for praise to God but also a reason for woe against themselves. And all this is because they know now that they murdered the Son of God, that their sin nailed the Savior to the tree. Therefore, they mourn over their sin to their dying day.

I have tried to give you a deeper understanding of true repentance than you had before. I trust that you have truly repented unto life and can say, "Thank God that I threw away my weapons of proud rebellion by repenting of my sin. Thank God that I looked to Jesus Christ and received Him to be my Savior from first to last!" But if you have not, listen carefully to me now: If I have spoken fables to you or fiction or dreams, then reject my discourse. If I have spoken in my own name, who am I that you should care one whit what I think? But if I have written what the King of kings and Lord of lords proclaimed, that you should repent for the kingdom of God has come with Him—and I have—then I charge you by the living God, by the world's only Redeemer, and by the blood of His cross, obey His divine message if you would have eternal life. If you refuse it, your blood is on your own head forever.

Study Questions

1. Why is repentance necessary?

2. What is *repentance*?

3. How can we prove from the Scriptures that repentance is a gift of God?

4. What is the difference between worldly sorrow and godly sorrow?

5. What are three kinds of false repentance? How can we recognize them?

6. How can we describe true repentance?

7. Why is it reasonable for God to require us to repent?

8. Why is the divine command to repent an urgent matter for unconverted sinners?

9. How does the command to repent have continual force for the believer?

10. In which category would you place your own repentance, and why: (1) no concern about your sin; (2) turning away from God's word in despair; (3) fearing hell but not turning to Christ; (4) having truly repented in the past but now backsliding in sin without repentance; or (5) walking in regular repentance over all known sins?

CHAPTER 4

Faith in Jesus Christ

Simon Peter, a bondservant and apostle of Jesus Christ,

To those who have obtained like precious faith with us by the righteousness of our God and Savior Jesus Christ.

Grace and peace be multiplied to you in the knowledge of God and of Jesus our Lord, as His divine power has given to us all things that pertain to life and godliness, through the knowledge of Him who called us by glory and virtue, by which have been given to us exceedingly great and precious promises.

—2 PETER 1:1–4

God has not saved us in a haphazard way. He did not save us on the spur of the moment as an afterthought. No, our redemption played an essential and primary part in the purpose of God from all eternity. I delight to look back on the Lord's redeeming thoughts before all time and say of them, "These are ancient things." An eternity before the stars flew like sparks from the anvil of omnipotence at this world's creation, God had contrived the way for the redemption of His own. In the covenant council chamber of eternity, the divine persons of the sacred unity arranged the procedure of all-glorious grace, and today all things are wrought according to the purpose of God's eternal salvific will.

The foundation of redemption in time was securely laid in the eternal covenant of redemption, of which the Lord Jesus Christ is the foundation. Infinite love, infallible wisdom, and immutable faithfulness combined to lay the foundation of our salvation, which can never be moved. In accordance with God's eternal purpose, when Christ came two thousand years ago, He accomplished the full salvation of His people by His righteous life and death work at Calvary, and He rose bodily from death and today sits at the Father's right hand, where He makes continual intercession for them.

The previous three chapters have carried us through the first aspects of Christ's amazing, marvelous salvation, showing its orderliness and the application to us of its benefits. We noted that our individual salvation is grounded in God's effectual calling of us to Himself by His Spirit's regenerating work. In chapter 3 we dealt with our first response to God's effectual summons, our repentance unto life. Now I want to treat our second response to God's effectual summons, faith in Jesus Christ. As I observed previously, repentance unto life and faith in Jesus Christ are twins; we cannot say who the older brother is because they come into the soul together. But when elect sinners truly repent and place their faith in Jesus Christ, we say that they have been *converted*, for that is what conversion is. That is to say, conversion consists of true repentance unto life and true faith in Jesus Christ, and no one has been truly converted if he or she lacks either or both of them.

Some people mistakenly think that they are first to believe in God the Father. But belief in God the Father is an aftereffect of faith in Christ. We come to believe in the eternal love of God the Father as a result of trusting the precious blood of the Son. These people say, "I would believe in the Son if I knew that God had elected me." But this is coming to the Father first, for election is the Father's act, as Paul expressly teaches in Romans 8:29: "Whom [the Father] foreknew, He also predestined to be conformed to the image of His Son"; and one cannot come directly to Him, as Jesus taught: "No one comes to the Father except through Me" (John 14:6). Therefore, you cannot know that you are elect until you first believe on Christ the Redeemer. Then through the Redeemer, you can approach the Father and know that you are one of God's elect. We will first consider the origin of our faith in Christ. Second, we will reflect on the nature of saving faith, and third and finally, we will think briefly about the instrumental function of saving faith.

The Origin of Our Faith in Christ

The first thing to note is that 2 Peter 1:1–4 says that we obtained our precious faith in Christ as an aspect of everything else pertaining to life and godliness that God's power has given us, which means that faith in Jesus Christ is a gift of God procured by Christ's cross work and effected by the Holy Spirit's work of regeneration. Faith in Jesus Christ is represented everywhere in Scripture as a saving grace—that is, as a saving gift. Saving faith, as with repentance and "every [other] spiritual blessing in the heavenly places" (Eph. 1:3), was divinely provided for in election, procured for the elect by Christ's cross work, and actually wrought in them as the second effect of the Holy Spirit's regenerating activity, in conjunction with the ministration of God's word that came to the elect sinner in some true form by sermon, by tract, by witness, or by hymn. The following Scripture passages put the gift character of saving faith beyond doubt.

In Acts 13:46–48, Paul declared to the Jews of Pisidian Antioch after they had blasphemed the word of God, "Since you reject [God's word], and judge yourselves unworthy of everlasting life, behold, we turn to the Gentiles." Luke then reports that the Gentiles to whom Paul turned "were glad and glorified the word of the Lord. And as many as had been *appointed to eternal life* believed." Luke teaches here that, unlike the blaspheming Jews who repudiated the word of God and judged themselves unworthy of eternal life, the believing Gentiles received the word of God because God had appointed them for eternal life.

"The Lord opened [Lydia's] heart to heed the things spoken by Paul" (Acts 16:14). Clearly, Lydia's heart response to Paul's word was a faith response, but it was prompted by the Lord's regenerating work of opening, or enlightening, her heart to it. Also in Acts, Apollos "greatly helped those who had *believed through grace*" (18:27).

To the Ephesians Paul writes, "By grace you have been saved through faith, and that not of yourselves; it is the gift of God, not of works, lest anyone should boast" (Eph. 2:8–9). Even though *faith* is a feminine noun in the Greek and *that* is a neuter demonstrative pronoun, it is still entirely possible that Paul intended to teach that "faith," the nearest possible antecedent, is the antecedent of "that," and accordingly saving faith is the gift of God. It is permissible in Greek syntax for the neuter pronoun to refer antecedently to a feminine noun, particularly when it serves to render more prominent the matter previously referred to (see, for example, "to you of salvation, and that from God" [Phil. 1:28]; see also 1 Cor. 6:6). The only other possible antecedents to "that" are the earlier feminine noun "grace," which hardly needs to be defined as a "gift of God"; the nominal idea of salvation implied in the verbal idea "you have been saved," which Paul has already implied is a gift by his use of "grace," and which, like "grace" and "faith," is also feminine in Greek; or the entire preceding notion of salvation by grace through faith, which amounts to saying that faith, along with grace and salvation, is the gift of God. However the text is exegeted, when all its features are taken into account, the conclusion is still unavoidable that faith in Jesus Christ is a gift of God.

Finally, Paul writes to the Philippians, "To you it has been granted on behalf of Christ…to believe in Him" (Phil. 1:29). It has been granted to the Philippians to believe in Christ.

This faith does not grow in a person's heart by nature; it is a thing that is obtained through grace. It is not a thing that is developed in the process of education in our public school systems, by the example of our parents, or even by our best Reformed churches. It is a gift that is obtained by regeneration. All our good comes from outside us; only evil can be educed from within us. How this magnifies the grace of God, and how low this casts human nature! Think a moment: Is not faith in Christ a very simple thing, merely to depend on the blood and righteousness of Jesus Christ? Does it not seem to be one of the simplest of virtues, to be nothing and to let Christ be everything, to be still and to let Him work for you? Does that not seem to be the most elementary of all the Christian graces? Indeed, it is; and yet human nature is so fallen and so utterly undone that it cannot attain to even this rudimentary principle. The Lord Himself must not only open the gates of heaven to us at the last but also must open the gates of our hearts to faith at the first. It is not enough for us to know that He must make us perfect in every good work, but we also need to be taught that He gives us even the desire for Christ, and when this is given, He enables us to extend the hand of faith whereby Christ becomes our Savior and our Lord.

But note too that this divine gift of faith has a specific object—that is to say, we believe, Peter writes, in "the righteousness of our God and Savior Jesus Christ" (2 Peter 1:1). What a full object of faith this is! It is first a faith that regards Jesus Christ as *divine*. Carefully note Peter's words: "our God." The person who believes in Christ only as a great prophet or a great teacher does not have the faith that saves. Charity might make us hope for the Unitarians' happy future, but honesty compels us to condemn them as far as vital godliness is concerned. It doesn't matter how intelligent their conversation may be, how outwardly appealing their manners may be, how patriotic their spirit may be; since Unitarians reject Jesus Christ as very God, they will without doubt perish everlastingly because they do not have the faith given by the Holy Spirit's regenerating work.

We must not attempt to be more liberal than was the Lord Himself, who said, "Before Abraham was, I AM" (John 8:58); and "If you do not believe that I am He, you will die in your sins" (v. 24). I can make no allowance for one who receives Christ as a great prophet, even the greatest prophet, but who rejects Him as God. It is an atrocious outrage against common sense for people to profess to believe in Christ at all if they do not believe in His deity. For if He was not God, He was the greatest impostor who ever lived, with His many claims about who He was. I cannot imagine a man viler than one who would lead his followers to adore him as God without ever putting in a word by way of caveat to stop their idolatry. If He were not God, the atrocity of His having palmed Himself off on us, His disciples, as God puts aside altogether from consideration every virtue of His life. He would be the grossest of deceivers if He were not God. Either this, or He was a lunatic, as C. S. Lewis says, on the level of someone who thinks he is a poached egg.[1]

But mark, too, that our faith in Christ regards Him as *"our…Savior"* (2 Peter 1:1). As if the glory of His Godness might be too bright for us, Peter followed it with the gentler words "our…Savior." And

---

1. See C. S. Lewis, *Mere Christianity* (New York: MacMillan, 1952), 54–56.

this means that trusting Jesus Christ as God will save no one unless there is added to this belief a Spirit-wrought resting in Him alone as the great propitiatory sacrifice. You say, "But surely no one would accept His deity but deny His saving work!" Over a billion Roman Catholics do it every time they go to Mass, every time they say a Hail Mary, and every time they pray to their thousand saints. Jesus alone is humankind's Savior because He became a substitute for His guilty people. It was He who stood in the place of sinners. When the whole tempest of God's wrath could legitimately have spent itself on us, He endured it all for His elect. When the great whip of the law could have legitimately fallen on us, He bared His shoulders to the lash. When the cry was heard: "Awake, O sword," it was against Christ the Shepherd, against the man who was the eternal God's fellow, that it was lifted (Zech. 13:7). And because He thus suffered, He received authority from on high to become the sole Savior of people and to bring many sons to glory.

Now note in 2 Peter 2:1 the word *righteousness*. Ours is a faith in the righteousness of our God and Savior. The doctrine of justification by faith is under attack today. Certain divines are trying to diminish Christ's righteousness to make room for the Christian's righteousness as an essential aspect of the basis for his or her justification. These divines need to remember what Isaiah said about our righteousness: "All our righteousnesses are like filthy rags" (Isa. 64:6). They should also note what Paul said about our righteousness: "Not by works of righteousness which we have done, but according to His mercy [God] saved us" (Titus 3:5). Christ's righteousness alone, like a white robe, must be placed on us. And I have not obtained the precious faith that the Holy Spirit works in Christ's people at all but am an enemy and an adversary to Christ unless I receive Him as *Yahweh Tsidkenu* (the Lord is our righteousness). His perfect life is the life for me; it contains every virtue. In it there is not one spot or wrinkle. My faith takes His righteousness, and with it about me I am so beauteously, so perfectly arrayed that even the eye of God can see neither spot nor blemish in me.

So if you are conscious that the Holy Spirit has performed His regenerating work in you; if you are aware that a vital life principle is within you that was not in you when you were born the first time; if you know the folly of carnal confidence; if you have cast away all your own righteousness; if you have laid your hands on the head of Him who was slain for sinners; if you are now resting entirely on Christ as your substitute and in His righteousness, His intercession, and His merit as the divine Christ, then rejoice in the Lord without ceasing if that blessed Redeemer has become your Savior. If He delivered you from sin and passed by your transgressions, then you know that Peter's benediction in 2 Peter 1:2 comes to you across the centuries as full and as fresh as ever: "Grace and peace be multiplied to you." So much then about the origin of saving faith. It is a gift of God alone.

The Nature of Saving Faith

According to Scripture, saving faith consists of three constituent elements: knowledge, assent, and trust. Benjamin Warfield explains, "We cannot be said to believe or to trust in a thing or person of which we have no knowledge; 'implicit faith' in this sense is an absurdity. Of course we cannot be said to believe or to trust the thing or person to whose worthiness of our belief or trust assent has not been obtained. And equally we cannot be said to believe that which we distrust too much to commit ourselves to it."[2]

Knowledge

Each of these elements requires comment. With respect to *knowledge*, it is appropriate to think of this element as the cognitive foundation, or base, of saving faith. The Bible insists that "faith comes by hearing, and hearing by the word of God" (Rom. 10:17) and that people must "love…the truth, that they might be saved" (2 Thess. 2:10); it also speaks of "repentance, so that they may know the truth" (2 Tim. 2:25). In sum, saving faith is based on divine testimony. The Bible knows nothing of the modern notion that faith is the enemy of knowledge. The Bible grounds saving faith in propositional truth, and it repudiates such sentiments as, "It is when one cannot or does not know that

---

2. Benjamin Breckinridge Warfield, *On Faith in Its Psychological Aspects*, in *Biblical and Theological Studies* (Philadelphia: Presbyterian and Reformed Publishing, 1968), 402–3.

one can or must believe," and, "Since faith has nothing to do with facts, it does not matter what one believes as long as one is sincere." These sentiments are simply empty superstitions and amount to salvation by ignorance or by sincerity, which is no salvation at all.

They also fatally wound Christianity in the heart. To the contrary, the Bible glories and delights in knowledge and propositional truth as the foundation of true faith, and it characterizes faith devoid of knowledge as believing the lie that leads to condemnation (2 Thess. 2:11–12). Accordingly, the Bible often highlights the knowledge aspect of saving faith by employing the construction "believe that" followed by a propositional truth to indicate the content of saving faith:

> Without faith it is impossible to please Him, for he who comes to God must *believe that* He is, and that He is a rewarder of those who diligently seek Him. (Heb. 11:6)

> If you do not *believe that* I am He, you will die in your sins. (John 8:24)

> I said this, that they may *believe that* You sent Me." (John 11:42; see also 17:8, 21)

> *Believe Me that* I am in the Father and the Father in Me. (John 14:11)

> For the Father Himself loves you, because you…have *believed that* I came forth from God. (John 16:27; see also v. 30)

> These are written that you may *believe that* Jesus is the Christ, the Son of God, and that believing you may have life in His name. (John 20:31)

> If you…*believe…that* God has raised [Jesus] from the dead, you will be saved. (Rom. 10:9)

> We *believe that* Jesus died and rose again. (1 Thess. 4:14)

> Whoever *believes that* Jesus is the Christ is born of God. (1 John 5:1)

In this feature of saving faith, John Murray said, "lies the importance of doctrine respecting Christ. The doctrine defines Christ's identity, the identity in terms of which we entrust ourselves to him. Doctrine consists in propositions of truth."[3]

Assent

The second aspect of faith, *assent*, refers to the intellectual or cognitive conviction that the knowledge one has acquired about Christ is indeed factually true and that the provisions of the gospel of Christ correspond exactly to one's actual (not necessarily felt) spiritual needs. Without this element faith simply becomes mysticism, for to place one's trust in what one has heard or read about but does not believe to be true is simply an existential leap into the sea of absurdity.

We must realize that it is entirely possible for an unregenerate person to know the propositions of the gospel and to have a keen comprehension of how the several propositions contribute to the gospel proclamation as a whole and yet still not believe that these propositions are factually true or that they address the person's deepest spiritual needs. The German theologian Rudolf Bultmann (1884–1976), for example, had as good an intellectual grasp of the content of the New Testament as the most orthodox of theologians, but he denied that Jesus was born of a virgin or performed the mighty miracles ascribed to Him or died on the cross as a sacrifice for sin or rose from the dead. Instead, Bultmann replaced these gospel truths with twentieth-century existentialist philosophy.

Trust

Murray said, "As assent is cognition passed into conviction, so *fiducia* [*trust*] is conviction passed into confidence."[4] And it is this third element—trust—that is saving faith's characteristic act as sinners cognitively, affectively, and volitionally transfer all reliance for pardon, righteousness, and cleansing away from themselves and their own resources in complete and total abandonment to Christ, whom they joyfully receive and on whom alone they rest entirely as their Savior and Lord for their salvation. It is essential that faith include this third

---

3. John Murray, "Faith," in *Collected Writings of John Murray* (Edinburgh: Banner of Truth, 1976), 2:258.

4. Murray, "Faith," in *Collected Writings*, 2:258.

element. Otherwise, one's faith is the intellectual faith of demons who "believe that there is one God" (James 2:19) and Jesus is both the Son of God and their Judge (Matt. 8:29), but because they have no cognitive affection for Christ they rather cognitively hate Him and refuse to trust Him.

Biblical expressions as "looking unto Jesus" (Heb. 12:2), eating Jesus's flesh and drinking His blood (John 6:51, 54, 56), receiving Christ (Matt. 18:5; Luke 19:6; John 1:12; 1 Cor. 15:1; Col. 2:6), and coming to Christ (Matt. 11:28; 19:14; Luke 6:47; John 6:35, 37; 14:6) are also descriptive of the activity of faith in Christ.

Faith in Jesus Christ is not a natural reaction to the gospel; it is not native to the depraved human heart. Rather, the Bible teaches that faith in Christ is the inevitable, Spirit-wrought response of the elect to the gospel, an effect of the Holy Spirit's regenerating activity in conjunction with the ministry of the word. Even so, it is also a human act, just as repentance is a human act. Even though people cannot in themselves respond in saving faith to God's gracious overtures, saving faith and the divine promises of justification and sanctification do not become thereby a divine monologue in which people are mere telephones through which God addresses Himself. It is the regenerated person, not God, who believes in Christ. But the miracle and the sovereignty of grace are still there in the regenerated person's faith in Christ.

The Instrumental Function of Faith

The Reformers quite properly saw that it is not faith per se that saves, but Christ who saves through or by the instrumentality of the sinner's faith in Him. They learned that

> the saving power of faith resides…not in itself, but in the Almighty Saviour on whom it rests. It is never on account of its formal nature as a psychic act that faith is conceived in Scripture to be saving…as if this frame of mind or attitude of heart were itself a virtue with claims on God for reward. It is not faith that saves, but faith in Jesus Christ…. It is not, strictly speaking, even faith in Christ that saves, but Christ that saves through faith. The saving power resides exclusively, not in the act of faith or

the attitude of faith or the nature of faith, but in the object of faith; …we could not more radically misconceive [the biblical representation of faith] than by transferring to faith even the smallest fraction of that saving energy which is attributed in the Scriptures solely to Christ Himself.[5]

The Reformers' clear vision of the instrumental function of faith, with the real repository of saving power being Christ alone, came from their recognition that all Scripture represents saving faith not only as the gift of grace but also as the diametrical opposite of law keeping and as the only human response to God's effectual summons, which comports with grace.

With a glorious regularity, Paul pits faith against all law keeping, showing faith's character to be the diametrical opposite. Whereas keeping the law relies on human effort to render satisfaction before God, faith repudiates and looks entirely away from all human effort to the cross work of Jesus Christ, who alone, by His sacrificial death, rendered satisfaction before God for His people, which is explained in the following verses:

> By the deeds of the law no flesh will be justified in [God's] sight.…
> But now the righteousness of God apart from law is revealed.… The righteousness of God, through faith in Jesus Christ, [comes] to all and on all who believe. (Rom. 3:20–22)

> We conclude that a man is justified by faith apart from the deeds of the law. (Rom. 3:28)

> To him who does not work but believes on Him who justifies the ungodly, his faith is accounted for righteousness. (Rom. 4:5)

> For if those who are of the law are heirs [of Abraham], faith is made void. (Rom. 4:14)

> For Christ is the end of the law for righteousness to everyone who believes. (Rom. 10:4)

> A man is not justified by the works of the law but by faith in Jesus Christ. (Gal. 2:16)

---

5. Warfield, *On Faith*, 424–25.

> That no one is justified by the law in the sight of God is evident,
> for "the just shall live by faith." (Gal. 3:11)

> Not having my own righteousness, which is from the law, but
> [the righteousness] which is through faith in Christ. (Phil. 3:9;
> see also Rom. 4:2; Gal. 2:20–21; 5:4; Titus 3:5)

These verses make it plain that Paul clearly taught that justification is by faith alone (*sola fide*). And just as clearly, since Paul never represents faith as a good work—indeed, since Paul always sets faith over against works as the receiving and resting on what God has done for us in Christ and freely offers to us—then it is by faith alone that sinners are justified.

Finally, faith alone comports with a salvation by grace that excludes all human boasting. Paul is explicit that if salvation is to be effected by God's grace (undeserved favor) and is to exclude thereby all human boasting, it can be only by a faith that looks away from all the native human resources of the one believing to the Savior's work of satisfaction.

> [Salvation] is of faith that it might be according to grace.
> (Rom. 4:16)

> And if [a saved Jewish remnant is] by grace, then it is no longer
> of works ["works" for Paul is opposed to faith]; otherwise grace
> is no longer grace. (Rom. 11:6)

> You…attempt to be justified by law [the opposite of being justified by faith]; you have fallen from grace. (Gal. 5:4)

I recall how shocked I was to hear a well-known preacher of the gospel say, "I do not know why salvation is by faith in Jesus Christ. God just declared that is the way it is going to be, and we have to accept it because God said it." This preacher should have known why salvation is by faith. He should have known because Paul expressly declared, "[Salvation] is of faith that it might be according to grace" (Rom. 4:16).

Furthermore, only salvation by grace alone through faith alone in Christ alone excludes all human boasting:

> Where is boasting then? It is excluded. By what law? Of works?
> No, but by the law of faith. (Rom. 3:27)

> The base things of the world and the things which are despised
> God has chosen, and the things which are not, to bring to noth-
> ing the things that are, that no flesh should glory [or boast] in
> His presence. (1 Cor. 1:28–29)

If God permitted fallen creatures to intrude their human works into the acquisition of salvation to any degree, salvation would not be by grace alone and people would have reason to boast before Him. Salvation by grace and salvation by works are mutually and totally exclusive. In sum, because salvation is by grace, it must be by faith in Jesus Christ, the nature of which is to turn totally and continually away from our own works to the work of another, even Jesus, on our behalf.

The Westminster Shorter Catechism, question 86, summa-rizes well what I have been saying: "Faith in Jesus Christ is a saving grace, whereby we receive and rest upon him alone for salvation, as he is offered to us in the gospel." Along with true repentance, it is the divinely effected human response to God's effectual summons of the elect sinner into fellowship with His Son. It is effected, as is repentance, normally in conjunction with the ministry of the word of God and by the regenerating operations of God the Holy Spirit in the human spirit. Because of God's universal command issued to all people to repent (Acts 17:30), His universal invitation extended to all people to come to Him (Isa. 45:22; Matt. 11:28; Rev. 22:17), and the all-sufficiency of Christ's cross work to save His people, sinners need not fear that Christ will refuse to save them or not be able to save them if they repent and come to Him. In these great gospel verities resides the guarantee that Christ is able and willing to save every sin-ner who repents and believes. And as soon as the sinner, in response to God's effectual summons, turns from his sin and places his confi-dence in Jesus Christ and His vicarious cross work, "thereby uniting [him] to Christ in [his] effectual calling" (WSC 30), God the Father immediately justifies him, definitively sanctifies him, and adopts him into His family, aspects of our salvation that we will consider in com-ing chapters.

As I conclude this chapter, I urge this: just as it is with repentance unto life, it is the duty of every person to trust Christ. It can never be less than a duty to believe the truth about Jesus Christ. Some will deny this on the ground that people do not have the spiritual ability to believe in Christ. This is an error of massive proportions; *the measure of sinners' moral ability is not the measure of their duty.* There are many things people ought to do that they have lost the moral and spiritual ability to do. A man ought to be chaste, but if he cannot restrain his passions, he is not thereby freed from the obligation. Every woman ought to believe that which is true, but if her mind has become so depraved that she loves a lie and will not receive the truth, is she thereby excused? If the demands of the law of God are to be lowered to the moral ability of sinners to keep them, then they would have to be reduced to zero, and sinners are under no rule at all, for they cannot keep any of them. No, the divine commands stand however incapable of faith people may be, and they are obligated to believe in Christ whether their sinfulness renders it impossible for them to do so or not. In every case it is people's duty to do what God commands them to do. And not to believe in Christ only adds sin to sin. So have you obeyed God by trusting His Son? I pray that you have.

Study Questions

1. Must we believe that the Father has loved and chosen us before trusting in Christ? Why or why not?

2. What is the origin of our faith in Christ?

3. Why must faith receive Christ as (1) our God, (2) our Savior, and (3) our righteousness?

4. Why is knowledge an essential element to saving faith in Christ?

5. What is *assent*? How is it an essential element to saving faith in Christ?

6. Why is trust in Christ necessary for salvation?

7. What is the instrumental function of faith in justification?

8. Why must salvation be through faith for it to be by God's grace alone?

9. Is it our duty to trust in Christ? How can this be if people lack the spiritual ability to believe in Him?

10. How would you assess your spiritual life with respect to each of the elements of faith in Christ: (1) knowledge, (2) assent, and (3) trust? Do you have all three? What is one area where you need to grow?

CHAPTER 5

Justification by Faith Alone

The gospel of Christ…is the power of God to salvation for everyone who believes, for the Jew first and also for the Greek. For in it [the good news of the gospel] the righteousness of God is revealed from faith to faith: as it is written, "The just shall live by faith."
—ROMANS 1:16–17

Therefore we conclude that a man is justified by faith apart from the deeds of the law.
—ROMANS 3:28

Therefore, having been justified by faith, we have peace with God through our Lord Jesus Christ.
—ROMANS 5:1

There is therefore now no condemnation [the antithesis to justification] to those who are in Christ Jesus.
—ROMANS 8:1

In 1483 the son of a miner, who was to do a great deal toward undermining the papacy and refining the church, was born into this wicked world. The name of that baby was Martin Luther, and he was a hero and a saint. The day of his birth bestowed a blessing on all succeeding ages, as this monk would shake the world. His brave spirit overturned the tyranny of error that had so long held nations in bondage. All human history since then has been affected by the birth of that marvelous boy. He was not an absolutely perfect man by any means, but he was a mighty judge in the Israel of God, a true servant of the Lord.

Luther unlocked the dungeons of the human mind and set at

liberty hearts held in bondage, and his golden key was the simple truth contained in Romans 1:17, "The just shall live by faith." This one sentence from Habakkuk 2:4 that Paul quotes produced the Reformation. Out of this one line came forth the sounding of gospel trumpets and the singing of gospel songs that were like the sounds of many waters. This one seed—forgotten, hidden away, and corrupted by the medieval church—dropped into Luther's heart and, by the Spirit of God, was made to grow and to produce great results for all times to come.

Luther could not be still about the simply stated truth, "The just shall live by faith." He had to speak it and write it and thunder it across the land. He abhorred doubts about it. Luther was the chief of dogmatists when it came to justification by faith alone. The times needed a firmly assured leader, and God made Luther a giant, a man of splendid mental capacity and strong physique whose faith had laid hold of the cross of Christ as his sole hope. He would not be moved from it. He cast his anchor on this truth of Holy Scripture alone and rejected all the inventions of clerics and false traditions of the fathers. May we all be as committed to this doctrinal truth that I bring before you in this chapter.

This truth is that the very second Spirit-regenerated sinners repent unto life and place their trust in Christ, God immediately does three things *for*—not in—them: He justifies them, definitively sanctifies them, and adopts them into His family. This chapter answers the question, What is the Christian's relation to God as lawgiver and judge? It declared that God has juridically acquitted him of any and all transgressions of the law and that he has been delivered forever from the wrath of God. Chapter 6, on definitive sanctification, answers the question, What is the Christian's relation to God as his new master? It declares that he is no longer sin's slave and is now the slave or servant of God. Chapter 7, on adoption, addresses the question, What is the Christian's relation to God Himself? And it declares that God is his heavenly Father, that he is a child of God and a member of His household. It is the first of these three divine acts that we will consider here, the doctrine of justification by faith alone.

When we take up the doctrine of justification by faith alone, we should be aware that we have come to the heart and core of the gospel, for the gospel is the good news that God by grace alone justifies sinners through faith alone in Christ's work apart from the works of the law. John Calvin declared that justification by faith alone is "the main hinge on which religion turns"[1] and "the sum of all piety."[2] The centrality of justification by faith alone in the Christian gospel is borne out by the fact that when Paul began to elucidate the "gospel of God" (Rom. 1:1) to which he had been set apart and of which he was not ashamed, declaring that "*in* it the righteousness of God is revealed from faith to faith" (v. 17), he did so precisely in terms of justification by faith alone. Consequently, we must take great care when elucidating this precious doctrine lest we wind up declaring another gospel. For example, we occasionally hear *justification* popularly defined as God "looking at me just as if I'd never sinned." This is an example of a very partial truth becoming virtually an untruth since nothing is said in such a definition concerning the ground of justification or the instrumentality through which justification is obtained. Much more accurately, the Westminster Shorter Catechism, question 33, defines justification as "an act of God's free grace, wherein he pardons all our sins, and accepts us as righteous in his sight, only for the righteousness of Christ, imputed to us, and received by faith alone."

Justification as a Legal Judgment

That *justification* is an objective forensic judgment, as opposed to a subjective transformation, is evidenced first by the meaning of the term itself in the following contexts.

Deuteronomy 25:1 says, "If there is a dispute between men, and they come to court, …the judges may judge them, and they justify the righteous and condemn the wicked." In justifying the righteous man, the judges were not *making* the man righteous; rather, they were *declaring* him to be what the evidence presented in the case demanded.

In Job 32:2 Elihu expresses his opinion that Job is arguing his

---

1. Calvin, *Institutes*, 3.11.1.
2. Calvin, *Institutes*, 3.15.7.

innocence before God—that is, declaring himself righteous before God: "Then the wrath of Elihu…was aroused against Job; his wrath was aroused because he justified himself rather than God."

Proverbs 17:15 is directed toward the judges of the land: "He who *justifies* the wicked, and he who *condemns* the just, both of them alike are an abomination to the LORD" (see also Ex. 23:7; Isa. 5:23). The judge who for a bribe (see Prov. 17:23) declared the wicked man to be righteous or who declared the righteous man to be guilty in either case provoked the Lord to anger.

Jesus speaks to the multitudes in Luke 7:29, "and when all the people heard Him, even the tax collectors justified God"; that is, they declared or acknowledged God to be just; they quite obviously did not make Him so (see also 10:29; 16:15).

A second evidence that justification is an objective forensic judgment, as opposed to a subjective transformation, is that the antithesis of justification is invariably condemnation, which is clearly a juridical or forensic determination. For example,

> They [shall] justify the righteous and condemn the wicked.
> (Deut. 25:1; see also Prov. 17:15)

> Judge Your servants, condemning the wicked…and justifying
> the righteous." (1 Kings 8:32; see also 2 Chron. 6:23)

> For by your words you will be justified, and by your words you
> will be condemned. (Matt. 12:37)

> The judgment which came from one offense resulted in con-
> demnation, but the free gift which came from many offenses
> resulted in justification. (Rom. 5:16)

> It is God who justifies. Who is he who condemns?
> (Rom. 8:33–34)

And that justification is an objective forensic judgment, as opposed to a subjective transformation, is evidenced, third, when the act of justifying is placed in the context of legal judgments. For example,

> Do not enter into judgment with Your servant, for in Your sight
> no one living is righteous [that is, shall be justified]. (Ps. 143:2)

> Now we know that whatever the law says, it says to those who
> are under the law, that every mouth may be stopped, and all the
> world may become guilty before God. Therefore by the deeds of
> the law no flesh will be justified [that is, declared righteous] in
> His sight. (Rom. 3:19–20)

> Who shall bring a charge against God's elect? It is God who
> justifies. (Rom. 8:33)

This biblical evidence makes it clear and places beyond all legitimate controversy that justification is a juridical or forensic determination made by a judge.

The Righteousness of Justification

In contrast to the official Roman Catholic teaching of the Council of Trent that the righteousness of justification is the "sanctification and renewal of the inward man,"[3] whereby the Christian is being inwardly made increasingly righteous through the impartation of sanctifying grace, stands the biblical, Protestant insistence that the righteousness of justification neither comes through any efforts on our part nor is infused or generated in us by the Holy Spirit. Rather, the righteousness of justification, as has already been stated, is the objective God-righteousness of Jesus Christ that God the Father, in the very act of justifying ungodly people, imputes to them, thereby constituting them legally righteous in His sight. This is a constituting act that no human judges can do when a guilty party stands before them.

This is why we are Protestants, because we take seriously the little words of the Bible as well as the big words, specifically the little word *one*: "By *one* Man's obedience many will be made righteous [justified]" (Rom. 5:19). Quite correctly did Luther declare that the Pauline doctrine of justification by faith alone is the article by which the church stands or falls. And by expressly rejecting this teaching as it did at the Council of Trent, which it not only has never repudiated but also has reaffirmed as recently as its 1994 Catechism of the Catholic Church,

---

3. Council of Trent, Sixth Session, First Decree, chap. 7, http://traditionalcatholic .net/Tradition/Council/Trent/Sixth_Session,_First_Decree.html.

the Roman Catholic Church testifies to its own apostate condition.[4] And in rejecting this doctrine, Rome has fallen heir to numerous other evils, including its indulgence system and its doctrines regarding the mass, works of supererogation by those whom it has determined have become "saints," whose "congruent merit" is placed in Rome's "treasury of merit," which merit is then dispensed through papal indulgences to the "faithful" as they submit to the Romish priesthood and its sacraments, the confessional and as prayers are offered in behalf of souls in a contrived, nonexistent purgatory.

That the righteousness of justification is the God-righteousness of the divine Christ Himself, which is imputed or reckoned to us the moment we place our confidence in Him, is amply testified to when the Scriptures teach that we are justified

- in Christ (Isa. 45:24–25; Acts 13:39; Rom. 8:1; 1 Cor. 6:11; Gal. 2:17; Phil. 3:9);

- by Christ's death work (Rom. 3:24–25; 5:9; 8:33–34);

- not by our own righteousness but by the righteousness of God (Isa. 61:10; Rom. 1:17; 3:21–22; 10:3; 2 Cor. 5:21; Phil. 3:9); and

- by the righteousness and obedience of Christ (Rom. 5:17–19).

In short, the ground of justification is the perfect God-righteousness of Christ that God the Father imputes to all sinners who place their confidence in the obedience and satisfaction of His Son. Said another way, the moment sinners, through faith in Jesus Christ, turn away from every human resource and rest in Christ alone, the Father imputes His well-beloved Son's preceptive (active) obedience to them and accepts them as righteous in His sight. And sinners who are now Christians may sing thereafter, in the words of Horatius Bonar,

---

4. *Catechism of the Catholic Church* (Vatican City: Libreria Editrice Vaticana, 1993), secs. 1987–95, Vatican, https://www.vatican.va/archive/ENG0015/__P6Y .HTM. See Council of Trent, Sixth Session, Canons 9–12, http://traditionalcatholic .net/Tradition/Council/Trent/Sixth_Session,_Canons.html.

Not what my hands have done
Can save my guilty soul,
Not what my toiling flesh has borne
Can make my spirit whole.
Not what I feel or do
Can give me peace with God,
Not all my prayers and sighs and tears
Can bear my awful load.

Thy grace alone, O God,
To me can pardon speak;
Thy power alone, O Son of God,
Can this sore bondage break.
No other work save Thine,
No other blood will do;
No strength save that which is divine
Can bear me safely through.

Justification properly understood, in contrast to Rome's tragically defective definition and representation, says nothing about the subjective transformation that will necessarily begin to occur within the Christian's inner life through the progressive infusion of grace that commences with the new birth. Scripture views this subjective transformation as progressive sanctification. Rather, justification refers to God's wholly objective, wholly forensic judgment concerning sinners' standing before the law, by which God declares that sinners are righteous in His sight because of the imputation of their sin to His Son, on which ground they are pardoned, and the imputation of His Son's perfect obedience to sinners, on which ground they are constituted righteous before God. In other words, for "him who does not work but believes on Him who justifies the ungodly" (Rom. 4:5), God pardons him of all his sins (Acts 10:43; Rom. 4:6–7) and constitutes him righteous by imputing the righteousness of Christ to him (Rom. 5:1, 19; 2 Cor. 5:21). And on the basis of His constituting the ungodly person righteous by His act of imputation, God simultaneously declares the ungodly person to be righteous in His sight.

What Justification Means to Those in Christ

The doctrine of justification means, then, that in God's sight the ungodly person, now in Christ as the result of the Spirit's regenerating work, has perfectly kept the moral law of God, which also means in turn that in Christ she has perfectly loved God with all her heart, soul, mind, and strength and her neighbor as herself.

It means that saving faith is directed to the doing and dying of Christ alone and not to the good works or inner experience of the believer.

It means that the Christian's righteousness before God is in heaven at the right hand of God in Jesus Christ and not on earth within the believer.

It means that the ground of our justification is the vicarious work of Christ for us, not the gracious work of the Spirit in us.

It means that the faith-righteousness of justification is not personal but vicarious, not infused but imputed, not experiential but judicial, not psychological but legal, not our own but a righteousness alien to us and outside of us, not earned but graciously given through faith in Christ, which is itself a gift of grace.

It means also in its declarative character that justification possesses an eschatological dimension, for it amounts to the divine verdict of the final judgment being brought forward into time and rendered here and now concerning the sinner. By God's act of justifying them through faith in Christ, sinners, as it were, have been brought, before the time, to the final assize and have already passed successfully through it, having been acquitted of any and all charges brought against them. Justification, then, properly conceived, contributes in a decisive way to the Reformation doctrine of the saint's eternal preservation and to his or her final glorification.

What a satisfying doctrine this is to the Christian's heart! It teaches us that we are not guilty before the high tribunal of heaven. A verdict of "not guilty" amounts to an acquittal, and the prisoner is immediately discharged. Christians receive their justification the moment they close with Christ and receive Him as their all in all. They are as truly and as fully justified as those who walk in white and sing God's praises above. The thief on the cross was justified the moment he turned the eye of faith to Jesus, and Paul the aged, after years of service, was not more justified than was the thief who offered no service at all. We are *today* accepted in the Beloved, *today* absolved from sin, *today* innocent in the sight of God. There are some clusters on the vine of salvation that we will not be able to gather until we get to heaven, but this is a cluster that we may pluck and eat here. Some of the corn of the land we will not be able to eat until we cross the Jordan, but this is manna in our wilderness; it is part of our daily raiment that God supplies us on our journey to the promised land. We are *now* pardoned. Even *now* are our sins put away. Even *now* we stand in the sight of God as though we had never been guilty. Even *now* there is not one unpaid sin in the Book of God against us, for Christ's blood has written, "It has been paid in full" across the Mount Everest-high pile of sins and evils, iniquities, and transgressions that we have committed against God. Even *now* nothing is laid to our charge. Even *now* in the sight of the Judge of all the earth there is neither speck, nor spot, nor wrinkle, nor any such thing remaining on those who have placed their trust in Christ. What ravishing, soul-transporting thoughts are these!

Not only is all this true of us now, but it will also be continually true of us. The moment we first trusted Christ, God said of us, "They are not condemned." Many days have passed since then for some of us, and we have seen many changes, but God still says of us, "They are not condemned." God alone knows how long our appointed days will be here before, like a shadow, we flee away. But this we know: though we should all live to be one hundred, God will still say, "They are not condemned." And if by some mysterious act of providence our lives should be lengthened to ten times the usual limit of mankind, should we even come to the 969 years of a Methuselah, God will still say the same of us: "They are not condemned." Christ declared, "I give [My sheep] eternal life, and they shall never perish; neither shall anyone snatch them out of My hand" (John 10:28).

These promises show that the justification that faith effects and that God pronounces will last as long as we live and will last throughout eternity as well. We will not wear in heaven any other dress than what we are wearing now. Today justified saints stand clothed in the righteousness of Christ, and they will wear the same wedding dress at the great wedding feast. And there is no chance that our present righteousness before God will ever lose its virtue because it is an eternal righteousness. The Lord is our righteousness (see Jer. 23:6; 33:16), and He is the self-existent, everlasting, immutable God whose years will know no end, whose strength will never fail, and whose perfections and beauty will know no termination.

Our justification is not only now and continual, but it is also complete since it is grounded in the work of Christ completely and is in no sense in our works. Our justification is not now and never will be partly of God's grace and partly of our works. If it is of our works to any degree, then it is not of grace; if it is of grace, it cannot be of our works to any degree. Divine grace and human works cannot mix and mingle any more than can fire and water. It is either one or the other; it cannot be both. Those who have trusted Christ are free from all iniquity, guilt, and blame, and should the devil bring an accusation, it will have no standing in God's court of law. We stand before God not half innocent but perfectly and completely so; not half washed but white—indeed, whiter than snow. All our sins have been erased and blotted out. They have been cast into the depths of the sea; they have been removed from us as far as the east is from the west. The book of Hebrews teaches that the ancient Israelites never had a conscience free from sin. After one sacrifice they needed still another, for these sacrifices could never make the sinner perfect. The next day's sin needed a new sacrifice, and next year's would need a new victim to make atonement. But, the writer to the Hebrews declared, "this Man, after He had offered one sacrifice for sins forever, sat down at the right hand of God" (10:12). No more burnt offerings are needed, no more blood, no more atonement, no more sacrifices, and definitely no Roman Masses. Your sins sustained their deathblow in Him; the robe of your righteousness received its last thread. It is complete, perfect; it needs no addition. It can never suffer any diminution.

Not only is our justification complete; it is also effectual. It will never miscarry. It is not a matter of theory; it is a matter of fact. You know that God's condemnation of the sinner is a matter of fact. When you and I had the heavy hand of the law of God placed on us, we knew that its curse was no mock thunder but was very real. We knew that the anger of God was indeed a thing to be trembled at. Just as real as the condemnation that justice brings is the justification that God's mercy bestows. You are not only nominally guiltless; you are really so if you trust in Christ. You are not only nominally put in the place of the innocent; you are really innocent the moment you believe in Jesus. Not only does God say that your sins are gone; they *are* gone. Not only does God look on you as though you were accepted; you *are* accepted. Your justification is as much an effectual matter of fact as the reality that you have sinned against God is a matter of fact. You do not doubt or deny that you have sinned. Then do not doubt that when you trusted God's Son, He pardoned you of all your sins and declared you to be continually, completely, and forever righteous in His sight.

Think about it: you are actually and effectually cleared from guilt. You have been led out of prison. You are no more in the fetters of a bondslave. You are no longer in bondage to the law as a covenant of works, and you can walk at large as God's free person. You have a right to come to your Father's throne. No flames of vengeance are there to scare you now; no fiery sword is slashing back and forth to keep you from approaching Him, for justice cannot smite the innocent. At one time you were unable to talk to your Father, but now you can. You had no right to speak to Him nor did He speak to you except with thunder, for you were a child of wrath—that is, one whom He could only consider with displeasure. But now you have access with boldness to His throne of grace. Once you feared hell, but there is no hell for you now; only a new earth under a new heaven awaits you. Once God frowned at you as an avenging God, but how can the righteous Judge now frown at the guiltless?

All the love and acceptance that a perfectly obedient being could ever obtain from God are yours because Christ kept the law perfectly for you. Christ was perfectly obedient on your behalf, and God has imputed Christ's infinite merit to your account that you might be exceedingly rich through Him who for your sake became exceedingly poor (2 Cor. 8:9). Our justification is so effectual that it puts us actually higher above where we would have been if we had never sinned. It fixes our standing before God more securely than it was before Adam fell. We are not now where Adam was, for Adam might fall and perish. Adam was placed in the garden under probation. We are not now and never will be under probation. There is no probation to determine whether children of God should be saved. They are saved already; their sins are washed away. Their righteousness is continual, complete, and effectual, and that righteousness could endure an eternity of probation and never be defiled if they were to be placed under probation.

All this is ours because God implanted within us His gift of faith in Jesus Christ. Consider again, as in the previous chapter, that our faith in Him lays hold of the righteousness of God by accepting His plan of justifying sinners through the work of Christ alone. That faith appropriates the whole system of divine righteousness revealed in the person and work of the Lord Jesus. That faith rejoices to know that Christ came into the world in our nature, and in that nature, He obeyed the law in every jot and tittle, even though He was not under that law until He willingly, voluntarily, lovingly placed Himself under it, offering Himself up as a perfect atonement and making a complete vindication of divine justice by His sufferings and death. That faith lays hold of Christ's work alone as the sinner's sole hope, and in the righteousness of Christ, it arrays the believer. That faith moves the believer, and here I am getting ahead of myself in this series of chapters, to everything that is right and good and true. That faith is the greatest sin killer under heaven. That faith in the constraining love of Christ moves the Christian to seek after everything that is acceptable in the sight of God. That faith trusts God, and therefore the believer loves God and obeys and grows into Him.

Christian, lay hold of these precious thoughts. I am not able to state the truth of your justification except in such weak terms, but do not let my weakness prevent your apprehending the glory and preciousness of your justification. It is enough to make believers leap for joy, though their legs be shackled in irons, and to make them sing, though their mouth be gagged and their lips covered with duct tape, to think that we are perfectly accepted in Christ, that our justification is not partial but goes the whole way in acquitting us. With Nicholaus Ludwig von Zinzendorf we can sing,

> Jesus, Thy blood and righteousness
> My beauty are, my glorious dress;
> 'Midst flaming worlds, in these arrayed,
> With joy shall I lift up my head.
>
> Bold shall I stand in Thy great day;
> For who aught to my charge shall lay?
> Fully absolved through these I am
> From sin and fear, from guilt and shame.

And with Augustus Toplady we can also sing:

> Fountain of never-ceasing grace,
> Thy saints' exhaustless theme,
> Great object of immortal praise,
> Essentially supreme.
> We bless Thee for the glorious fruits
> Thine incarnation gives;
> The righteousness which grace imputes,
> And faith alone receives.
>
> In Thee we have a righteousness
> By God himself approved;
> Our rock, our sure foundation this,
> Which never can be moved.
>
> As all, when Adam sinned alone,
> In his transgression died,
> So by the righteousness of One
> Are sinners justified.

Now I will summarize and conclude. I have contended that Paul defined the "gospel of God," which is also the "gospel of His Son" (Rom. 1:1, 9), Christ, specifically in terms of justification by faith alone in the accomplishments of Christ's obedience and cross work, completely apart from all law keeping (Rom. 1:16–17; 3:21–22, 27–28; 4:5–8; 5:1, 9, 17–19). And the manner in which he employs the term indicates that he regarded justification as an objective divine acquittal respecting the sinner's status before the condemning law of God, and not as the sub-jective improvement of the sinner through the infusion of sanctifying grace. This was not only the gospel that Paul explicated in Galatians and Romans but the gospel that he preached: "Through this Man," he proclaimed in Acts 13:38–39, "is preached to you the forgiveness of sins; and by Him everyone who believes is justified from all things from which you could not be justified by the law of Moses." And he pronounced an anathema on any and all who would muddy the river of grace that makes glad the city of God by their legalistic efforts to contribute in any way to their righteousness before God (Gal. 1:6–9; 2:11–21; 3:1–14; 5:1–4; 6:12–16). J. I. Packer has written that the biblical doctrine of justification

> defines the saving significance of Christ's life and death by relating both to God's law (Rom. 3:24ff.; 5:16ff.). It displays God's justice in condemning and punishing sin, his mercy in pardoning and accepting sinners, and his wisdom in exercising both attributes harmoniously together through Christ (Rom. 3:23ff.). It makes clear what faith is—belief in Christ's atoning death and justify-ing resurrection (Rom. 4:23ff.; 10:8ff.), and trust in him alone for righteousness (Phil. 3:8–9). It makes clear what Christian moral-ity is—law-keeping out of gratitude to the Savior whose gift of righteousness made law-keeping needless for acceptance (Rom. 7:1–6; 12:1–2). It explains all hints, prophecies, and instances of salvation in the OT (Rom. 1:17; 3:21; 4:1ff.). It overthrows Jewish exclusivism (Gal. 2:15ff.) and provides the basis on which Chris-tianity becomes a religion for the world (Rom. 1:16; 3:29–30). *It is the heart of the gospel.*[5]

---

5. J. I. Packer, "Justification," in *Evangelical Dictionary of Theology*, ed. Walter A. Elwell (Grand Rapids: Baker, 1984), 593.

Study Questions

1. How did God use Martin Luther to start the Reformation?

2. What is *justification*?

3. How does the Bible show that justification is a legal judgment, not a personal transformation?

4. What does the Roman Catholic Church teach about the righteousness of justification?

5. What is the righteousness given in justification?

6. What does justification mean for those who are in Christ?

7. Why is it satisfying for the Christian to know that he is justified now and forever?

8. How would you explain that justification by faith is complete and effectual?

9. What precious truths about justification can we glean from the hymns "Jesus, Thy Blood and Righteousness" and "Fountain of Never-Ceasing Grace"?

10. What reasons does the doctrine of justification by faith alone give a believer to rejoice in the Lord? Are you rejoicing in this truth? Why or why not?

CHAPTER 6

Definitive Sanctification by Faith Alone

…among all those who are sanctified.
—ACTS 20:32

…those who are sanctified by faith in Me.
—ACTS 26:18

…those who are sanctified in Christ Jesus.
—1 CORINTHIANS 1:2

For when we were in the flesh, the sinful passions which were aroused by the law were at work in our members to bear fruit to death. But now we have been delivered from the law, having died to what we were held by, so that we should serve in the newness of the Spirit and not in the oldness of the letter.
—ROMANS 7:5–6

As has been noted, the moment regenerate sinners place their trust in Christ's atoning work, God does three things for them: He justifies them, definitively sanctifies them, and adopts them into His family. *Justification* means that God acquits believers of all transgressions of the law so that they are delivered forever from the wrath of God. When God definitively sanctifies believers, they are no longer sin's slave and are now the slave of God. Third, God adopts believers and becomes their heavenly Father, so that they are children of God and members of His household. It is the second of these marvelous deeds of God that we will consider now, so let us delve into our definitive sanctification in greater detail.

Sanctification as God's Definitive Act

The Christian faith has represented *sanctification* as a process that begins with the Spirit's regeneration and continues throughout the Christian's life, and there can be no question that in a very real sense it is, as we shall soon see. But there is solid biblical evidence for viewing sanctification as also a definitive (punctiliar, or relating to a point in time) act of God following on His act of definitively (punctiliarly) justifying repentant, trusting sinners, to which their progressive sanctification should conform. The biblical evidence for the definitiveness of sanctification, in addition to the verses cited at the beginning of the chapter, include "Such were some of you. But you were…sanctified" (1 Cor. 6:11); and "Christ also loved the church and gave Himself for her, that He might sanctify and cleanse her" (Eph. 5:25–26). These references employ the aorist tense, which is generally used for an action occurring at a point in time or an action completed—not processive—action, to describe Christians. There are also numerous instances when Christians are called saints—for example, in Ephesians 1:1; Philippians 1:1; and Colossians 1:2.

So we can see that the New Testament often represents Christians as those who have already been sanctified, whom God has already set aside as sacred to Himself, and therefore who have already been definitively constituted in some way and on some basis as holy.

In addition to the biblical statements offered above, I would also call your attention to the following verses or passages as additional evidence for God's definitive sanctification of the believer:

We…*died* to sin. (Rom 6:2)

Our old man *was crucified* [with Christ]. (Rom. 6:6)

You *were* slaves of sin…. And *having been set free* from sin, you *became slaves* of righteousness….

You *were* slaves of sin…. But now *having been set free* from sin, and *having become slaves* of God…. (Rom. 6:17, 18, 20, 22)

You also have become dead to the law…. For…we *were* in the flesh…. But *now* we have been delivered from the law, *having died* to what we were held by. (Rom. 7:4–6)

We, *having died* to sins, might live for righteousness. (1 Peter 2:24)

Therefore, since Christ suffered for us in the flesh, arm your-selves also with the same mind, for he who has suffered in the flesh [a reference to the Christian who "suffered in the flesh" when Christ "suffered in the flesh"] has ceased from sin, that he no longer should live the rest of his time in the flesh for the lusts of men, but for the will of God. (1 Peter 4:1–2)

What do these biblical affirmations of our death to sin and the law mean? For our answer we will turn to the passage we considered ear-lier in Romans 7. Paul draws an exceedingly interesting and striking parallel between the relationship of a wife to her first husband, on the one hand, and the relationship of the Christian to the law who was his or her first husband, on the other hand. He begins this parallel with a question: "Do you not know, brethren…, that the law has dominion over [literally, "lords it over"] a man as long as he lives?" (v. 1). To illustrate his point, Paul observes that a wife is bound to her husband as long as he lives, and she can only marry again without committing adultery if her husband dies. Should he die, she is no longer bound to her husband and is free to marry another without committing adul-tery. Why is this so? The second marriage is legitimate because the husband's death has terminated the first marriage. We will see that the way Paul applies the principle of verse 1 presupposes an extension of it—namely, that the law concerning marriage between two persons is binding only while *both* are alive. Should either partner die, that marriage is no longer in force, and the other partner is free to marry again. Now in Romans 7:4–6 comes Paul's application: just as death terminates the marriage bond, so also our death has terminated our bondage to the realm of law that gives sin its power (see also 1 Cor. 15:56). But how did we die?

Paul's language intends that since the fall, every son and daugh-ter of Adam comes into this world like a woman who is married to her husband, even the law of God; that is to say, every child of Adam comes into the world under obligation to obey God's law, his or her first husband. But while this husband is "holy and just and good" (Rom. 7:12), he does not love and is incapable of loving his wife. All he can do is issue commands to her and condemn her if she disobeys him. He can only help her to obey him with promises that he will let her live if she obeys him perfectly and with threats of punishment and death at her slightest infraction. Thus, he cannot "impregnate" her so that she is able to bring forth living offspring. Indeed, by his constant issuing of commands, he enflames her sinful passions to disobedience (Rom. 5:20; 7:5, 7–25). So all her offspring—that is, all her deeds—are stillborn, or in Paul's language, "fruit to death" (Rom. 7:5).

But Paul argues that the Christian's relationship to the domain of law as the first husband has been terminated. How? "Through the body of [the slain] Christ" (Rom. 7:4), so that he or she could be and has been united to another husband, even to Christ, who was raised bodily from the dead, who loves His bride, who forgives her when she disobeys Him, and who is able by His Spirit (I speak reverently when I say this) to "impregnate" her with spiritual seed so that she is able to and desires to bring forth living fruit for God. This means that when Christians sin, they are no longer disobeying their first husband as a covenant of works; they are disobeying their second husband. But what a difference there is between the two husbands! The second husband—that is, Christ—unlike the first, loves His wife, freely forgives her, and empowers her by His infused love for her to want to obey Him.

While admittedly Paul's illustration contains an inversion of the stated principle—for the wife dies rather than the husband because Paul could not say that the law, as the first husband, died, which would be an error because the law continues even for the Christian as the covenant norm of morality for daily life. Rather, he says that Christians die "through the body of [the slain] Christ" (v. 4) to their first husband, the law, as the means to obtaining righteousness, and their death results in the same thing—namely, the termination of that first marriage relationship. Paul's meaning is plain enough: if sinners are ever to live as God would have them live, they must somehow die to the domain of law as a covenant of works and become the bride of another, even the bride of the living Christ, who is able to and will assist His bride to live uprightly. The Christian did this—that is, he or she died—Paul declares, "through the body of [the slain] Christ." But how is it that he or she died to the law "through the body of [the slain] Christ"? What does Paul mean here?

By the language of our death to sin and of our liberation from slavery to sin, the Bible depicts a radical contrast between believers' pre-Christian existence and the life they now live as a Christian. The Bible affirms that Christians are not only definitively justified, but they are also made definitively holy the moment they trust Christ. The Bible affirms that the Christian died with Christ to sin and has been liberated from the domain of law, from which sin derives its power. Accordingly, the Scriptures speak often of every Christian as a "holy one" or as a "saint." This sustained contrast can only mean that for the Christian there exists, states John Murray,

> a cleavage, a breach, a translation as really and decisively true in the sphere of moral and religious relationship as in the ordinary experience of death. There is a once-for-all definitive and irreversible breach with the realm in which sin reigns in and unto death.... In respect of every criterion by which moral and spiritual life is to be assessed, there is absolute differentiation. This means that there is a decisive breach with the power and service of sin in the case of everyone who has come under the control of the provisions of grace.[1]

In sum, not only does God look at believers as righteous in His sight, but He also looks at them as definitively holy in His sight.

The Ground of the Christian's Holiness

What is the ground of the Christian's definitive breach with sin and his or her definitive holiness? It should come as no surprise when I say that just as the ground of the Christian's once-for-all-time justification before God is Christ's imputed righteousness, a saving benefit all Christians receive from God the Father the moment they become a partaker of Christ through faith in Him, so also the ground of the Christian's definitive sanctification, or holiness, is real spiritual union with Christ in His crucifixion, death, burial, and resurrection (Rom. 6:1–14; 2 Cor. 5:14–15), into which saving union believers are actually brought the moment they become partakers of Christ through faith in Him. In other words, just as Christians are accounted by God the

---

1. John Murray, "Definitive Sanctification," in *Collected Writings*, 2:279–80.

Father in His definitive justification as righteous in regard to the law, so also they are constituted holy by God the Father in His definitive sanctification through their spiritual union with Christ in regard to the power and mastery of sin. As I stated in *A New Systematic Theology of the Christian Faith*:

> Union with Christ is the fountainhead from which flows the Christian's every spiritual blessing…. Chosen in Christ before the creation of the world, and *in the divine mind* united with Christ in his death and resurrection, the elect, in response to God's effectual call, are through God's gift of faith *actually* united to Christ. Their union with Christ is in no sense the effect of human causation…. By virtue of his actual union with Christ the Husband in his death and resurrection, the Christian, as Christ's "bride," is forgiven of his sin and liberated from the law—his previous "husband"—and made capable of doing that which he could never do before, namely, "bear holy fruit to God" (Rom. 7:4–5). To the degree that the Christian "reckons himself dead to sin but alive to God in Christ Jesus" (Rom. 6:11), that is to say, to the degree that the Christian takes seriously the reality of his Spirit-wrought union with Christ, to that degree he will find his *de facto* definitive sanctification coming to actual expression in his experiential or progressive sanctification. The holiness of the Christian's daily walk directly depends upon his union with Christ.[2]

Some theologians have contended that the verses I cited above are simply describing what they call the Christian's position in Christ as God views him or her. But I must insist that it is not simply positional holiness that these verses envision but a real, existential breach with the reign and mastery of sin that is created by the Christian's actual spiritual union with Christ in His crucifixion, death, burial, and resurrection, a breach that is as decisive and definitive as are Christ's crucifixion, death, burial, and resurrection. We should not overlook that Paul's discussion in Romans 6:1 begins with this question: "Shall we continue in sin that grace may abound?" He is asking a practical

---

2. Robert L. Reymond, *A New Systematic Theology of the Christian Faith*, 2nd ed. (Grand Rapids: Zondervan, 2020), 739.

question in response to the objection that arose from his insistence that Christians are justified by faith in Christ completely apart from works of law—namely, the objection that contended his doctrine of justification by faith alone apart from works of law grants Christians license to sin. And he responds to his practical question: "Certainly not!" That is, Christians are not to practice sin. Then he asks a second question: "How shall we who died to sin live any longer in it?" (v. 2). And he explains how it is that we died to sin and live now to God by appealing to our spiritual union with Christ in His crucifixion, death, burial, and resurrection. His answer is not merely affirming the Christian's position in Christ as God sees him or her; rather, it sets forth in a very practical way the ground of the Christian's existential death to sin in actual experience.

This spiritual union of the Christian with Christ, about which Paul speaks with a glorious monotony, "embraces the wide span of salvation from its ultimate source in the eternal election of God to its final fruition in the glorification of the elect. It is not simply a phase of the application of redemption; it underlies every aspect of redemption both in its accomplishment and in its application."[3] For proof of this statement, see Paul's scores and scores of "in Christ" statements sprinkled throughout his writings and the striking figures he employs to illustrate the believer's spiritual union with Christ, such as the relation of stones in a building to the building's foundation and chief cornerstone (Eph. 2:19–22), the relationship between members of a body and the body's head (4:15–16), and the relationship between a wife and her husband (5:22–23). Because the Holy Spirit causes and maintains the bond of our spiritual union with Christ, its reality must not be doubted. It must be taken seriously because *your union with Christ is as real as if there were a literal umbilical cord uniting Him to you and you to Him, reaching from Christ in heaven to you on earth.* That is how real it is! I must say this because not only are Christians' growth in grace (Rom. 6:1–14) and hope of glory (Col. 1:27) grounded in their spiritual union with Christ, from whom they derive by the

---

3. John Murray, *Redemption Accomplished and Applied* (Grand Rapids: Eerdmans, 1989), 165.

Holy Spirit all their strength and power to live the Christian life (2 Cor. 12:9), but also their existence as Christians in the first place.

John Murray explicates the significance of the vital spiritual union between Christ and believers for their definitive sanctification in the following words:

> So intimate is the union between Christ and his people, that they were partakers with him in [His crucifixion, death, burial, and resurrection], and therefore died to sin, rose with Christ in the power of his resurrection, and have their fruit unto holiness, and the end everlasting life.... The decisive and definitive breach with sin that occurs at the inception of Christian life is one necessitated by the fact that the death of Christ was decisive and definitive. It is just because we cannot allow for any reversal or repetition of Christ's death on the tree that we cannot allow for any compromise on the doctrine that every believer has died to sin and no longer lives under its dominion. Sin no longer lords it over him. To equivocate here is to assail the definitiveness of Christ's death. Likewise the decisive and definitive entrance upon newness of life in the case of every believer is required by the fact that the resurrection of Christ was decisive and definitive. As we cannot allow for any reversal or repetition of the resurrection, so we cannot allow for any compromise on the doctrine that every believer is a new man, that the old man has been crucified, that the body of sin has been destroyed, and that, as a new man in Christ Jesus, he serves God in the newness which is none other than that of the Holy Spirit of whom he has become the habitation and his body the temple.[4]

I am not advocating by this doctrine of definitive sanctification that Christians actually achieve, personally and existentially, sinless perfection the moment they trust Christ; this would leave no room for progressive sanctification. Besides, entire sanctification awaits the coming of our Lord Jesus Christ (1 Thess. 5:23). And Christians who say they have no sin are deceiving themselves, and the truth is not in them (1 John 1:8). But I am advocating here—indeed, insisting

---

4. Murray, "The Agency in Definitive Sanctification," in *Collected Writings*, 2:289, 293.

on it—that all Christians, the moment they become a Christian, by virtue of their union with Christ, are instantly constituted a saint, enter into a new relationship with respect to the former reign of sin in their life and with God Himself in which they cease to be slaves to sin and become servants of God and of Christ. And Christians must and will take this breach with sin, constituted by their union with Christ, as seriously as God does and stop presenting their "members as instruments [that is, as servants] of unrighteousness to sin" and start presenting themselves "to God as being alive from the dead, and [their] members as instruments [that is, as servants] of righteousness to God" (Rom. 6:13).

In sum, in Romans 6:1–14 the apostle Paul argues that our practical conquest of our personal sins will occur

- as we *know* of our definitive death to sin and newness of life in Christ;

- as we *believe* these things to be true of us; and

- as we *act* in accordance with it—that is, as we *stop* presenting the members of our bodies to sin "as instruments of unrighteousness" and *start* presenting ourselves to God as those "alive from the dead," and our "members as instruments [or servants] of righteousness to God" (v. 13).

When we do this, we have Paul's assurance that "sin shall not have dominion over [us]" (Rom. 6:14).

So, rejoice in the truth that God considers you, by virtue of your real and vital union with Christ, definitively holy in His sight. Glory that He no longer sees you as slaves of sin but as His and your Savior's servants. Believe it to be true, and conform your lives to the definitive holiness that is true of you.

Study Questions

1. What is *definitive sanctification*?

2. What is the difference between definitive sanctification and progressive sanctification?

3. Where is definitive sanctification taught in the Holy Scriptures?

4. What does Paul teach about definitive sanctification by the analogy of a woman's marriage in Romans 7?

5. How did John Murray describe definitive sanctification?

6. What is the ground of the Christian's definitive sanctification?

7. What is *union with Christ*?

8. How is union with Christ not merely a positional truth but a powerful reality?

9. According to Romans 6, how can we experience the practical conquest of our sins?

10. How has reading this chapter helped you to pursue holiness through faith in Christ?

CHAPTER 7

Adoption

When the fullness of the time had come, God sent forth His Son, born of a woman, born under the law, to redeem those who were under the law, that we might receive the adoption as sons.

And because you are sons, God has sent forth the Spirit of His Son into your hearts, crying out, "Abba, Father!" Therefore you are no longer a slave but a son, and if a son, then an heir of God through Christ.
—GALATIONS 4:4–7

You did not receive the spirit of bondage again to fear, but you received the Spirit of adoption by whom we cry out, "Abba, Father." The Spirit Himself bears witness with our spirit that we are children of God, and if children, then heirs—heirs of God and joint heirs with Christ.
—ROMANS 8:15–17

We…who have the firstfruits of the Spirit, even we ourselves groan within ourselves, eagerly waiting for the adoption, the redemption of our body.
—ROMANS 8:23

[God the Father] in love…predestined us to adoption as sons by Jesus Christ to Himself.
—EPHESIANS 1:4–5

The moment regenerated sinners place their faith in Jesus Christ, God pardons and constitutes and declares them righteous in His sight and declares, by virtue of their union with Christ, that a radical breach now exists between them and sin's mastery. The former of these divine acts the Bible terms *justification*, as we have seen, and the latter of these divine acts the Bible represents as *definitive sanctification*. Now we take up our adoption, which follows our justification and our definitive sanctification, for God would never adopt one into His family who is not righteous and holy. This speaks to the filial relationship of Christians to God as their Father, declaring that God is their heavenly Father, Christ is their elder brother, and they are children of God.

The four passages cited at the opening of the chapter provide a beautiful biblical theology of adoption. Follow me and see if you do not agree. In love the Father predestined us to adoption in Christ before the foundation of the world. Then the Father sent His Son into the world to accomplish the redemptive work necessary both for the salvation of His people and for their elevation by adoption out of the tutelary discipline of the Mosaic economy under which they had lived in former times as minors to the status of full, mature sons. The Father also sent forth His Spirit of adoption into the hearts of believers, subjectively assuring them that they are the children of God and enabling them to cry, "Abba, Father." Finally, the children of God, having received the Spirit as the firstfruits of their adoption, await the final stage of their adoption in the eschaton when their mortal bodies will be redeemed from incorruption and are brought to the state of glory like that of their Lord. Thus conceived, adoption encompasses the Father's love from all eternity, redemption from past enslavement, the status of sonship in the present age, and the future expectation of full glory, of both soul and body.

Privileges of Sonship

The term *adoption* envisions an action on the Father's part that is legally constituting and not subjectively transforming in character. The status of sonship is legally bestowed on believers by their adoption, which is the apex and epitome of redemptive grace and privilege. Paul suggests the exalted status that adoption envisions in Ephesians 1:5 when he relates the Christian's adoption back to the Father's predestinating love. Here we have in one verse the ultimate source of grace, God's predestination, and the highest privilege of grace, adoption, brought together. Neither justification nor definitive sanctification, as great as these privileges are, can supersede the blessedness of being adopted children of the holy God.

This sonship involves both privileges and responsibilities. Time would fail me if I attempted to itemize the long list of our joyous privileges. Does our Father adorn the lily of the field and will we go naked? No, He arrays us with the robe of our Savior's perfect righteousness. Does He feed the birds of the air and will we feel necessity? He feeds us. As God's children, we Christians also have the Father's name placed on us (Eph. 3:14–15), being assured thereby that we have our Father's protection. We also are sealed by the Holy Spirit (Eph. 1:13; more on this to come). And we immediately become Christ's brothers and sisters; Christ Himself is the "firstborn among many brethren" (Rom. 8:29), and we now are "heirs of God and joint heirs with Christ" (v. 17), with our inheritance that is imperishable and undefiled and that will not fade away awaiting us in heaven, being assured that we will come into our inheritance because God is keeping us through faith for the "salvation ready to be revealed in the last time" (1 Peter 1:4–5). We also have ready access to our Father's throne of grace, and we can pray, "Our Father in heaven."

Those who can pray that are something more than just creatures; they have been adopted into God's family. He has taken them from the old family in which they were born. He has washed them and given them a new name and a new spirit, and He has made them His heirs and coheirs with Jesus Christ His Son. And He did all this out of His own free and sovereign, unmerited, distinguishing grace. And you may be assured that if God the Father has adopted you, He loves you. How He loves you and me! He is the best of fathers.

Those of you who are parents have some sense of how much you love your children. When your daughter is sick, you stand by her sickbed and pity her as her little frame writhes in pain. Like a father pities his children, so the Lord pities those who fear Him. You know, too, when one of your children grieves you because of his sin how your anger arises and you are ready to chasten, but no sooner is the tear in his eye than your hand stays, and you feel you would rather smite yourself than smite him. Jeremiah tells us that God "does not afflict willingly" or "grieve" His children (Lam. 3:33). Is that not a sweet thing to know? Even though God is compelled to do it at times, He takes no pleasure in chastening us. It is only His great love and deep wisdom that bring down the blow.

But you will know your love for your children most if one of them dies. David knew he loved his son Absalom, but he never knew how much he loved him until he heard that he had been killed. "Precious in the sight of the LORD is the death of His saints" (Ps. 116:15). God knows how deep and pure is the love that death can never sever. But you do not know and cannot tell how unfathomably deep the love of God for you, His child, is. As you consider the heavens, the moon and the stars that He has made, you ask with David, "What is man that You are mindful of him?" (Ps. 8:4). And you will marvel that while He owns all these marvelous treasures, He should set His heart not on them but on such insignificant creatures as you and me and love us to death—to the death of His Son in your stead.

Think about this high privilege, child of God. You can call God your Father. His name is on you, and you belong to His family. Quite interestingly, according to Galatians 4:6, the Spirit comes crying, "Abba, Father," and according to Romans 8:15, He enables us to cry "Abba, Father." Commentators such as William Hendriksen and F. F. Bruce have explained the expression as meaning that we are the ones who cry, "Abba, Father," and it is true according to Romans 8:15 that we who have "received the Spirit of adoption" do cry, "Abba, Father." But the text in Galatians does not say this—it says the Spirit, too, cries "Abba, Father"—and we are not at liberty to alter it on any pretense, and we will surely lose some aspect of the truth that God intends if we do so. So how are we to understand this? The Spirit of the Son comes to our hearts crying, "Abba, Father," as our teacher, prompting us who are now sons and daughters of God to cry, "Abba, Father," as Romans 8:15 teaches. But it is His cry first because He suggests it, approves it, inspires it, and educates us to it. As parents teach children to speak as they should by saying again and again, "Listen to me and to my words and repeat after me," so our teacher the Spirit puts these words continually in our hearts and on our lips. In sum, we would never have known to cry "Abba, Father" if the Spirit of God had not first taught us to do so. He puts that cry in the hearts of all believers because it is His educating cry first.

Moreover, it has often been said that these two words—the first Aramaic, the second Greek—are intended to remind us that both Jews and Gentiles are one before the Father. While they do remind us of this, this is not the reason for their use. This cry is literally the cry of the Son of God Himself in Mark 14:36. The second evangelist alone, who makes striking points with memorable words, records that our Lord prayed in the garden of Gethsemane, "Abba, Father, all thing are possible for You. Take this cup away from Me; nevertheless, not what I will, but what You will." Are we to think that Christ used both words in His agonizing prayer because Jews and Gentiles are one? Why should He have thought of that doctrine, and why did He need to allude to it in this pleading prayer to His Father? Some other reason must be suggested for His use of these words, and it seems to me that it is this: our Lord said "Abba, Father," because it was His native language. If I am right, then the Spirit of adoption is showing us that we should use the language of the heart, our native tongue, when we pray and that we are to be very natural with God, not stilted and formal, and should speak freely to Him. We should speak affectionately with our Father and come close to Him in our prayers with warm words fitting those of a little child looking into the face of his father.

Note, as well, that we *cry*, "Abba, Father." If we were to obtain an audience with an earthly king or dignitary, we would not cry but would speak in measured tones and set phrases. But the Spirit of adoption breaks down our measured tones and takes away the formality that some hold in great admiration, and He leads us to cry to God, which is the very opposite of formality and stiffness. A cry is not a sound that we would want every passer-by to hear. Yet what child minds if her father hears her cry? So when our hearts are broken and subdued, we should not feel that we must speak in fine language, but the Spirit sends forth from our hearts cries and groans, and we should not be ashamed of these nor should we be afraid to cry before God. Some of you may think that God does not hear your prayers because you cannot pray grandly. But God will hear your broken language, your words salted with grief and wet with tears. Go to Him with holy familiarity, and do not be afraid to cry in His presence. For when you cry before God, it is evidence of your earnestness and fervency. A cry is not a flippant utterance nor a mere thing of the lips. It comes from the soul. Did not our Lord teach us by His parable of the importunate widow to cry to God with fervency that will not accept denial? Has He not brought us so near to Him that sometimes we want to say, "I will not let You go except You bless me!" (see Gen. 32:22–26). We should cry out after Him, our heart and our flesh crying out for the living God. And this is what we cry: "Abba, Father, we must know You, taste Your love, dwell under Your wing, and feel Your great fatherly heart overflowing and filling our hearts with peace."

The stranger to God cannot understand the nearness of the believer's soul to God and to Christ, and because the world does not understand this, it finds it easy to sneer at Christians as emotional wackos, but what of that? We know that if we came to God only as our judge, we would have no right to expect that He would hear us favorably, but He would have every right to say, "You are transgressors of My laws; be gone." If we came to Him only as our king, He could say, "You are rebellious subjects; go away." If we addressed Him only as our creator, He could well say, "Yes, and I am sorry that I made you." If we called him only our preserver, He could justly say, "Yes, I have pre-served you, but you have shown your thanks by rebelling against Me."

But when we approach Him as our Father, all our sins cannot invalidate our claim on Him as our Father through Jesus Christ. He loves us with a father's love, and poor though our speech may be, He will not despise us. We have no fear that He will not understand us if we get our words out of order or split our infinitives or fail to finish a sentence; He understands our meaning anyway. Though our prayers should be as little broken things that we cannot put together, He will hear us. Though we have to say with David, "Lord, all my desire is before You" (Ps. 38:9)—not our words but our desire—we know that our Father still understands us. A dear brother prayed in a prayer meeting, "Lord, I cannot put my words together tonight; I cannot pray as I should. But Father, you know my meaning," and sat down. That is real prayer, and you should pray, dear ones, until the real you is pray-ing to the real God who is your Father in heaven.

I mentioned above the sealing of God's Spirit. The Spirit of God's Son who is also the Spirit of adoption not only testifies with our spirits that we are children of God but also, as the guaranteeing pledge (the down payment, if you like) of our inheritance, He seals us as God's possession to the day of eschatological redemption (Eph. 4:30). Paul deals with this topic in two places.

First, in Ephesians 1:13–14 he writes, "Having believed, you were sealed with the Holy Spirit of promise, who is the guarantee of our inheritance until the redemption of the purchased possession, to the praise of His glory." Note should be taken here that the Spirit's sealing, as with justification, definitive sanctification, and adoption as a whole, follows the Christian's believing as another of the immediate consequences of faith. Note, too, that the Spirit's sealing is represented as an accomplished fact, doubtless occurring at the point of our adoption, suggesting that just as the indwelling Spirit is the witness that we are children of God and as such are heirs of God, so also the indwelling Spirit of adoption becomes the guaranteeing pledge of our full and final inheritance and the mark, or seal, that we belong to God's household.

Second, Paul writes in 2 Corinthians 1:21–22, "He who establishes us with you in Christ and has anointed us is God, who also has sealed us and given us the Spirit in our hearts as a guarantee." Paul says virtually the same thing here as in the previous passage: that the indwelling Spirit's sealing is an accomplished fact and is God's pledge of ownership that guarantees we are children of God forever. From these virtually identical statements we learn that, contingent on our faith in Christ, God not only justifies us, not only definitively sanctifies us, not only adopts us into His family, but also by the Spirit of adoption He seals us in Christ as Himself the guaranteeing deposit of our final glorious inheritance. What does this mean? The first thing I want to emphasize is that we are not speaking here about chronologically related events. The Spirit's sealing, as is true of justification, definitive sanctification, and adoption, does not follow trust in Christ chronologically. That is to say, people do not trust Christ one moment and the Holy Spirit seals them in Christ in the next. Rather, I am saying that faith in Jesus Christ is the instrumental cause of the sealing.

The moment people trust Christ, that same moment the Holy Spirit seals them in Christ. While the two acts occur simultaneously, the Spirit's sealing is contingent on the trust as the effect is on its cause.

It should be noted that the seal is the indwelling Spirit of adoption Himself. He Himself is the sealing pledge of our inheritance, becoming the seal marking God's ownership of the Christian and the authenticating pledge guaranteeing the Christian's inheritance of every spiritual blessing in heaven in Christ. These are our privileges.

Responsibilities of Sonship

As for our responsibilities as beloved children, we Christians should love God in return. We should rejoice in being in our Father's presence and delight to commune with Him. Children of God, shouldn't we, His chosen favorites, love our Father in heaven? Shouldn't we say, "Whom have we in heaven but You? And there is nothing on earth that we desire in comparison to You" (see Ps. 73:25). "Glorious Father, we will give You our hearts, and You will be our guide from our youth. Because You love us, You will have our hearts as Your own forever."

We should also trust our heavenly Father for our every need. This means that we should behave as children of God by living above fear, anxiety, and the vanities of this world. This means that we will bring all our needs to Him in prayer and leave them with Him.

We should also show childlike reverence, love, and zeal for our heavenly Father in everything. We should reflect habitually on His great glory and majesty. We should stand in awe of Him, rendering Him praise and thanksgiving in all things. We should heed Malachi 1:6:

> A son honors his father....
> If then I am the Father,
> Where is My honor?

This means that we should abandon all bad company, all our former sins and lusts, never to resume or to take them into our practice again, and our heavenly Father is to be our first reason for being, and His word becomes our law. Childlike reverence should overflow in love to Him. Such love will lead to zeal for your Father's glory. When we hear the world sneering at or see the world striking at our heavenly Father, our spirits should boil within us.

We should also obey Him. We should not rise up against Him in rebellion. If He is our Father, we should not reject His commands but reverently obey them. If He has said, "Do this," let us do it not because we dread Him but because we love Him. If He forbids us something, let us avoid it for the same reason. Some people who do not have the Spirit of adoption within them can never be brought to do a thing unless they see some advantage in it for them. They do what is called a virtuous act only because they hope to gain heaven or to avoid hell by it, but haven't they served only themselves when they think that way? And what is that but selfishness? But there is no such motive in the children of God. Never do they think, "If I do this good work, I will gain heaven by it"; nor do they think, "If I avoid this bad thing, I will avoid damnation." For children of God know that their good works do not make them acceptable to God, for they were acceptable to God before they had any good works. And the fear of hell does not affect them, for they know that they have been delivered from hell forever; they know that they will never come into condemnation, having passed from death to life. Children of God act from love for God and for His Christ and out of gratitude for what the triune God has done for them.

Children of God will want to be engaged in their Father's work. We will discipline ourselves and channel our energies into the structures and work that God has for us to do, both in the world and in the fellowship of His church.

We should also love, cherish, and encourage our brothers and sisters in Christ and walk in love. And as children of light, we are to walk in the light and expose the unfruitful works of darkness, never forgetting that we will experience our Father's displeasure and chastening love if we go astray.

In summary, the Westminster Shorter Catechism, question 34, defines *adoption* as "an act of God's free grace, whereby we are received into the number, and have a right to all the privileges of the sons of God." This simple definition informs us that adoption is the Father's objective determination concerning believers, determined on their faith in Christ and bestowed by His free grace to make them His children. Adoption is the highest privilege available to the fallen children of men, with all its privileges accruing to those who enjoy the status of being heirs of all the promises of God and of everlasting salvation, including access to the Father's throne of grace and His pity, protection, provision, and chastening, as well as the seal of His Spirit to the final day of redemption.

Study Questions

1. How do the four Scripture passages quoted at the beginning of this chapter provide a biblical theology of adoption?

2. What does God give to believers in the act of adoption?

3. How does adoption change our relationship to God the Father and Christ?

4. How can understanding adoption transform how a Christian views God in times of sickness and in death?

5. What does *abba* mean? What does it mean that the Holy Spirit cries, "Abba, Father" in the hearts of believers?

6. How would you explain the sealing of the Holy Spirit?

7. What responsibilities do God's children have toward Him because of their adoption?

8. What responsibilities do God's children have toward each other in light of their adoption?

9. How does the Westminster Shorter Catechism define *adoption*?

10. Do you believe that adoption by God is your highest honor and privilege? Why or why not?

CHAPTER 8

Progressive Sanctification

I am the LORD your God. You shall therefore consecrate yourselves, and you shall be holy; for I am holy…. For I am the LORD who brings you up out of the land of Egypt, to be your God. You shall therefore be holy, for I am holy.
—LEVITICUS 11:45

As He who called you is holy, you also be holy in all your conduct, because it is written, "Be holy, for I am holy."
—1 PETER 1:15–16

The Bible makes clear that the entire Godhead sets great store on real holiness in the people of God. Jude 1 says we have been "sanctified *by God the Father*," 1 Corinthians 1:2 tells us that we have been "sanctified *in Christ Jesus*," and 1 Peter 1:2 informs us that our salvation includes "sanctification *of the Spirit*." All three are coagents working to produce a church without spot or wrinkle. It should not have to be argued that the three persons of the Godhead are vitally engaged in every true (regenerate) Christian's progressive sanctification. Since it is true that the Christian life is lived according to the Holy Spirit (Rom. 8:5); since it is true it is by the Holy Spirit we set our minds on the things of the Spirit that bring life and peace to us (v. 6); and since it is true that it is by the indwelling Holy Spirit we put to death the sinful deeds of the body (v. 13), then it is surely true that God the Holy Spirit is involved in our sanctification.

Since it is true that it was God the Son who sent the Holy Spirit into the church on the day of Pentecost (Acts 2:33), proving thereby that He, the baptizer of His people, is both its Lord and Messiah, then it is true that the Son is involved in our sanctification. But since all this is true, it is no less true that this Pentecostal event in turn occurred in accordance with the "Promise of the Father" (Acts 1:4; see also 2:33); that God the Father sanctifies us in and by the truth of His word (John 17:17); and that it is the God and Father of our Lord Jesus Christ "who has blessed us with every spiritual blessing in the heavenly places" (Eph. 1:3). But God the Father does not bless us in sanctification apart from God the Son, in whom every blessing in heaven comes to us, or apart from God the Holy Spirit, who seals us by indwelling when we believe in Christ and who thereby becomes the guarantor of our inheritance (Eph. 1:13–14). Clearly, the entire Godhead is engaged in our growth in grace and holiness and in our knowledge of the triune God.

Holiness is the architectural plan upon which God builds up His living temple, and those who despise holiness of heart are in direct conflict with Him. We read in the Scriptures of the "beauty of holiness" (1 Chron. 16:29; 2 Chron. 20:21; Pss. 29:2; 96:9). Nothing is beautiful before God that is not holy. Never forget that. All the glorious splendor of Lucifer, the present god of this world, could not screen him from divine abhorrence when he defiled himself with sin. "Holy, holy, holy" (Rev. 4:8)—the continual cry of the seraphim standing above God's heavenly throne—is the loftiest praise that creatures can offer Him. God counts His holiness to be among His choicest treasures. It is the seal on His heart and the signet on His right hand. He could as soon cease to be God as cease to be holy.

So, we who profess to be His children also ought to set a high value on purity and godliness in our manner of life. Value the blood of Christ as the foundation of your hope indeed, but never speak disparagingly of the sanctifying work of the Spirit that makes you fit for the inheritance of the saints in light. Indeed, prize it! Prize His sanctifying work so heartily that you, with the triune Godhead, dread the very appearance of evil. Prize it so much that in your ordinary actions you will be "a holy nation, His own special people, that you may proclaim the praises of Him who called you out of darkness into His marvelous light" (1 Peter 2:9). God has declared that we are kings before Him in Christ. But we know very little about how kings who are bound for heaven should act. So He has told us that He is going to spend the rest of our lives teaching us by specific means how kings with this heavenly destiny should think, act, talk, pray, and worship, and this is carried on in what we call *perseverance*, by which the Christian is preserved and continues in a gracious state and is made to abound in good works.

The Old Testament makes clear in Exodus 19:6 that God set His people apart from the beginning for a special purpose: "You shall be to Me a *kingdom* of priests and a holy nation." But sanctification involves more than being merely set apart, for in Exodus 19:10–12 God told Moses to sanctify the people, which consisted in certain outward deeds by which their bodies and their clothing were brought into a clean state. So it also means to be actually clean and pure. And in Leviticus 19:2 we read, "Speak to all the congregation of the children of Israel, and say to them: 'You shall be holy, for I the LORD your God am holy,'" which is clearly a state of moral purity.

The primary New Testament word group that addresses this topic means the same thing—"to set apart for a special purpose" and "to be pure." Peter summons the Christian to holiness and cites the Old Testament command to be holy to fortify his demand: "But as He who called you is holy, you also be holy in all your conduct, because it is written, 'Be holy, for I am holy'" (1 Peter 1:15–16).

A significant noun meaning "holiness" is also employed in this connection. Note the following occurrences:

This is the will of God, your sanctification [i.e., holiness]: that you should abstain from sexual immorality. (1 Thess. 4:3)

God did not call us to uncleanness, but in holiness. (1 Thess. 4:7)

Pursue…holiness, without which no one will see the Lord. (Heb. 12:14)

Another significant noun specifying the Christian's obligation to perfect a holy walk is found in 2 Corinthians 7:1: "Let us *cleanse* ourselves from all filthiness of the flesh and spirit, perfecting holiness in the fear of God."

So there can be no question that God wants His people to be holy before Him.

Progressive Sanctification

We have been moving through the several aspects of the biblical order of application of Christ's accomplished redemption. In previous chapters we saw that our individual salvation begins with God's effectual summons of us into fellowship with His Son and into His kingdom. We saw that summons is made effectual in God's elect by the regenerating work of the Spirit of God whereupon sinners—now spiritually alive—repent of their sin and place their faith in Jesus Christ. The instant you trust Christ, as we have seen, God the Father justifies you, definitively sanctifies you, and adopts you into His family and seals you as His child forever. Also, the instant you are made alive in Christ in regeneration, the Holy Spirit commences the lifelong process of purifying you by giving you new life and conforming you more and more into the likeness of your elder brother, even the Lord Jesus Christ.

From the moment of your regeneration to the moment of your final elevation to heavenly glory, you—by virtue of the Spirit's regeneration, your vital spiritual union with Christ's death and resurrection, and through the power of God's word and Spirit dwelling within you—will necessarily experience progressive sanctification. This work is carried out in two ways: by *mortification*, sending death to that which is evil in you, and by *vivification*, giving life to that which is good within you. Or we can say that this work is to be understood negatively in terms of putting to death the deeds of the flesh that still remain in you and positively in terms of your growth in all the saving graces. Consider first the scriptural warrant for the negative side of progressive sanctification: "If by the [indwelling] Spirit you put to death the deeds of the body, you will live" (Rom. 8:13); and, "Put to death your members which are on the earth: fornication, uncleanness, passion, evil desire, and covetousness, which is idolatry" (Col. 3:5). It should be noted that both of these admonitions to Christians to put to death the evil deeds of the body follow immediately on Paul's insistence that they have died to sin (Rom. 6–7; Col. 3:3). Clearly, Paul expects Christians to conform their processive death to sin to their definitive death to sin.

The following nine verses or passages address the positive side of progressive sanctification:

Be transformed by the renewing of your mind. (Rom. 12:2)

We all, with unveiled face, beholding as in a mirror the glory of the Lord, are being transformed into the same image from glory to glory. (2 Cor. 3:18)

[Christ] gave [spiritually gifted men]…for the equipping of the saints…, for the edifying of the body of Christ, till we all come to the unity of the faith and of the knowledge of the Son of God, to a perfect man, to the measure of the stature of the fullness of Christ; that we should no longer be children…but…[we] may grow up in all things into Him who is the head—Christ—from whom the whole body, joined and knit together by what every joint supplies, according to the effective working by which every part does its share, causes growth of the body for the edifying of itself in love. (Eph. 4:11–16)

And this I pray, that your love may abound still more and more in knowledge and all discernment. (Phil. 1:9)

Brethren, I do not count myself to have apprehended [perfection]; but one thing I do, forgetting those things which are behind and reaching forward to those things which are ahead, I press toward the goal for the prize of the upward call of God in Christ Jesus. (Phil. 3:13–14)

We…do not cease to pray for you, and to ask [God] that you may be filled with the knowledge of His will…that you may walk worthy of the Lord…, being fruitful in every good work and increasing in the knowledge of God. (Col. 1:9–10)

May the Lord make you increase and abound in love to one another…, that He may establish your hearts blameless in holiness before our God and Father at the coming of our Lord Jesus Christ. (1 Thess. 3:12–13)

Desire the pure milk of the word, that you may grow thereby. (1 Peter 2:2)

Grow in the grace and knowledge of our Lord and Savior Jesus Christ. (2 Peter 3:18)

The New Testament clearly refuses to endorse a carnal Christian experience as a legitimate status quo. It envisions the Christian life simultaneously as one of dying and one of living—of dying more and more to sin and of living more and more to holiness.

A Threefold Standard of Holiness

The Scriptures do not leave the pattern according to which Christians are to conform their lives in any doubt. They set forth a distinct and unmistakable threefold standard of holiness according to which we should pattern our Christian walk—namely, the ethical holiness of God Himself, His preceptive will that is set forth in His law, and Christ's earthly walk. Let us look at this threefold standard in greater detail.

First, since man was created originally in God's image (Gen. 1:26–27) and, according to Paul, is re-created by grace according to God's image in knowledge and true righteousness and holiness (Eph. 4:24; Col. 3:10), the Scriptures summon us to emulate the ethical holiness of God Himself as He demands that we be holy as He is holy (Lev. 11:44–45; 19:2; 1 Peter 1:15–16). See also Christ's admonition, "You shall be perfect [in your mercy], just as your Father in heaven is perfect [in His mercy]" (Matt. 5:48; see also Luke 6:36); and Paul's expression "forgiving one another, even as God in Christ forgave you" (Eph. 4:32; see also Col. 3:13).

Second, biblical revelation defines that likeness according to which our lives are to be patterned concretely in terms of conformity to God's preceptive will—the moral law or Ten Commandments (Ex. 20:1–17; Deut. 5:6–21). That is to say, the Decalogue is the moral norm for the Christian's covenant way of life. Reformed Christians deny that the continuing normativity of the law places them under it as a covenant of works, insisting rather, in the words of Westminster Confession of Faith 19.5–7, that

> the moral law for ever binds all, as well justified persons as others, to the obedience therefore; and that, not only in regard of the matter contained in it, but also in respect of the authority of God the Creator, who gave it. Neither does Christ, in the Gospel, any way dissolve, but [does] much strengthen this obligation.

Although true believers are not under the law, as a covenant of works, to be thereby justified or condemned; yet is it of great use to them, as well as to others; in that, as a rule of life informing them of the will of God, and their duty, it directs and binds them to walk accordingly; discovering [revealing] also the sinful pollutions of their nature, hearts, and lives; so as, examining themselves thereby, they may come to further conviction of, humiliation for, and hatred against sin, together with a clearer sight of the need they have of Christ, and the perfection of his obedience. It is likewise of use to the regenerate, to restrain their corruptions, in that it forbids sin: and the threatening of it serve to show what even their sins deserve; and what afflictions, in this life, they may expect for them, although freed from the curse thereof threatened in the law. The promises of it, in like manner, show them God's approbation of obedience, and what blessings they may expect upon the performance thereof; although not as due to them by the law as a covenant of works. So as, a man's doing good, and refraining from evil, because the law encourages to the one, and deters from the other, is no evidence of his being under the law; and not under grace.

Neither are the forementioned uses of the law contrary to the grace of the Gospel, but do sweetly comply with it; the Spirit of Christ subduing and enabling the will of man to do that, freely and cheerfully, which the will of God, revealed in the law, requires to be done.[1]

Third, since Christ was "born under the law" (Gal. 4:4) and perfectly fulfilled all its precepts, and since conformity to the image of Christ is the Father's predestined end for believers (Rom. 8:29), it is little wonder that Christ, as the third pattern for Christian living, is set before believers as the supreme exhibit of the pattern of sanctification. Christ declares, "I have given you an example, that you should do as I have done" (John 13:15). Paul enjoins, "Let this mind be in you which was also in Christ Jesus" (Phil. 2:5). And Peter writes, "Christ also suffered for us, leaving us an example, that you should follow His steps" (1 Peter 2:21). As Christians, through Christ's enabling grace,

---

1. See also the extended expositions of the law of God in both the Larger (questions 93–148) and Shorter (questions 41–81) Catechisms.

"[behold] as in a mirror the glory of the Lord, [they] are being transformed into the same image from [one stage of] glory to [the next stage of] glory" (2 Cor. 3:18).

Agents Effecting Progressive Sanctification

What are the ordinary agents and instrumentalities that effect progressive sanctification? It is important to understand that you can no more sanctify yourselves by your own efforts than can you justify yourselves by your own works. As we have already noted, the Scriptures insist that it is the triune Godhead who must effect our sanctification by His own grace and power:

> John 17:17: When Jesus prayed: "Sanctify them by Your truth," it was the Father's aid and the Father's Word that He was invoking in behalf of His disciples' sanctification.

> Romans 8:13–14: "…if by the Spirit you put to death the deeds of the body, you will live. For as many as are led by the Spirit of God, these are sons of God." Here it is the Spirit of God who enables you to put to death the sinful deeds of the flesh.

> 1 Thessalonians 5:23: "…may the God of peace Himself sanctify you completely." Again, the referent of the phrase "the God of peace" is the Father.

> 2 Corinthians 3:18: "…we all…are being transformed…from glory to glory, just as [it comes] from the Lord of the Spirit [or perhaps "the Spirit of the Lord"]." Here the referent of the last phrase is either Christ or the Spirit of Christ.

Although growth in grace is divinely energized, I would not suggest for a moment that you are to be passive in your spiritual growth. To the contrary, you are to be fully and consciously engaged in your progressive sanctification. Peter calls upon you to be "diligent to make your call and election sure" (2 Peter 1:10) by practicing moral excellence, self-control, perseverance, godliness, and brotherly kindness (vv. 5–6); and Paul counsels that you should "work out your own salvation with fear and trembling" (Phil. 2:12). Pages could be filled with passages having this same emphasis. But in the context where Paul urges Christians to work out their own salvation, he reminds them that they do so "for it is God who works in you both to will and to do for His good pleasure" (v. 13). John Murray appropriately comments here:

> God's working in us is not suspended because we work, nor our working suspended because God works. Neither is the relation strictly one of co-operation as if God did his part and we did ours so that conjunction or coordination of both produced the required result. God works in us and we also work. But the relation [between God's work and our work] is that *because* God works we work. All working out of salvation on our part is the effect of God's working in us, not the willing to the exclusion of the doing and not the doing to the exclusion of the willing, but both the willing and the doing.[2]

So the triune God is the agent of our sanctification. The Spirit of God creates a new heart and a right spirit within us and works in us to produce the fruit of the Spirit (Gal. 5:22–23). Never, never forget this. It will be a bad day when we begin to think lightly of the work of the Holy Spirit. We delight to magnify the work of Christ for us, but we must equally delight in the work of the Holy Spirit within us.

Moreover, just because our sanctification is ultimately effected by the triune God, we may not "grow negligent, as if we were not bound to perform any duty unless upon a special motion of the Spirit; but we ought to be diligent in stirring up the grace of God that is in us" (WCF 16.3). Not only should we in faith obediently be about the business of fulfilling our normal duties and responsibilities as Christian husbands, wives, parents, children, employers, and employees simply because we know God expects it of us, but also we should in faith actively avail ourselves of the ordinary means or instrumentalities of grace that God provides for our spiritual growth. And what are they? Chief among them are the following.

First is the reading and especially the preaching of the word of God. Jesus said in John 17:17, "Sanctify them by Your truth. Your word is truth." Paul declared in Acts 20:32, "Now…I commend you to God and to the *word of His grace*, which is able to build you up and give you an inheritance among all those who are sanctified."

---

2. Murray, *Redemption Accomplished and Applied*, 148–49.

How important it is, then, that truth be preached from church pulpits. Elders and church members must never tolerate a ministry that plays fast and loose with the great doctrines and great precepts of the gospel of grace. Divine truth is the sanctifier, and if you do not hear the truth and depend on it, you will not grow in holiness. You will only progress in sound living as you progress in sound understanding. The psalmist declares, "Your word is a lamp to my feet and a light to my path" (Ps. 119:105). Never say of error, "It is a mere matter of opinion." For if it is treated as a matter of opinion today, it will become a matter of practice tomorrow. Every grain of truth is a grain of diamond dust, so prize each one.

Second is the receiving and attendance on the sacraments of the church. Paul informs us in Galatians 3:27, "As many of you as were baptized [by the Spirit] into Christ have put on Christ," which spiritual truth the sacrament of baptism signifies. In Romans 6:3, 11 he writes

> Do you not know that as many of us as were baptized [by the Spirit] into Christ Jesus were baptized into His death?…
>
> Likewise you also, [in light of your baptism into Christ's death] reckon yourselves to be dead indeed to sin.

Third is prayers of adoration, confession, thanksgiving, and supplication. Paul exhorts in Philippians 4:6, "Be anxious for nothing, but in everything by prayer and supplication, with thanksgiving, let your requests be made known to God." John affirms in 1 John 5:14, "Now this is the confidence that we have in Him, that if we ask anything according to His will, He hears us." And practical James in James 4:2 declares, "You do not have because you do not ask." This is the reason that you attend as often as you can the times that your church sets aside for prayer.

Fourth is the fellowship of the saints in their gathered assemblies. Luke tells us in Acts 2:42, 46 that the early Christians "continued steadfastly in the apostles' doctrine and fellowship, in the breaking of bread, and in prayers…. So continuing daily with one accord in the temple, and breaking bread from house to house, they ate their food with gladness and simplicity of heart." Accordingly, Paul writes in Hebrews 10:24–25, "Let us consider one another in order to stir up love and good works, not forsaking the assembling of ourselves together, as is the manner of some, but exhorting one another, and so much the more as you see the Day approaching."

Finally are all of the providences of life that God works together to perfect in us that which He has predestined for us—namely, our conformity to the image of His Son (Rom. 8:28–29, 35–39), including the "all things" he mentions in Romans 8.

In summary, progressive "sanctification is the work of God's free grace, whereby we are renewed in the whole man after the image of God, and are enabled more and more to die unto sin, and to live unto righteousness" (WSC 35). It is transparently plain from all of Scripture that God desires, in accordance with His holy calling by which we were called, that you, His people, be holy before Him. And His people will so walk. For just as there is no sanctification that is not preceded by justification, so also there is no justification that is not followed by sanctification. The scriptural demand for and its expectation of holiness in the Christian should stir any professing Christians in whom there is no hungering and thirsting after righteousness to examine to see if he is actually in the faith (2 Cor. 13:5).

This is not to say that God's people will not experience conflict with sin and temptation. Galatians 5:17 assures us that we will struggle with the flesh. But we are also assured that "through the continual supply of strength from the sanctifying Spirit of Christ, the regenerate part does overcome; and so, the saints grow in grace, perfecting holiness in the fear of God" (WCF 13.3). The greatest need Christian children have is to see their parents walking with Christ in holiness before them. The greatest need a congregation has is to see its pastor and its officers living in true piety before it. And the greatest need of the church today is a holy walk before the Lord. So strive for practical holiness, because without that you will not see the Lord. Do not let anyone ever say of you, "There is a Christian, but he (or she) is no better than other people."

Study Questions

1. How is each person in the Trinity involved in the progressive sanctification of God's people?

2. Why should we treasure holiness?

3. What are some Scripture passages that show God's desire for His people to be holy?

4. What is *progressive sanctification*?

5. What is *mortification*? Where is it taught in the Bible?

6. What is *vivification*? Which Scripture passages teach it?

7. What is the threefold standard of holiness?

8. What personal agents are the cause of sanctification?

9. What instruments (or means) has God provided for the sanctification of His people?

10. Are you engaged in the work of sanctification? If not, why not? If so, how can you make better use of the means of sanctification to grow in holiness?

CHAPTER 9

Perseverance of the Saints

Being confident of this very thing, that He who has begun a good work in you will complete it until the day of Jesus Christ.
—PHILIPPIANS 1:6

The dangers that attend the spiritual life are of the most appalling kind, and the life of a Christian is a series of miracles. See a spark living in mid-ocean, see a stone hanging in midair, see health blooming in a leper colony, and see a snow-white swan swimming in a river of filth, and you get some idea of the Christian life. The new nature is kept alive in the very jaws of death and is preserved by the power of God from instant destruction. And by no power less than divine does its existence continue. Instructed Christians see their surroundings and find themselves like a defenseless dove flying to its nest while tens of thousands of arrows are leveled against it. The Christian's life is like that dove's anxious flight as it threads its way between death-bearing shafts of the enemy, and by constant miracles it escapes unhurt. Enlightened Christians see themselves to be like a traveler standing on the narrow summit of a lofty ridge; on the right hand and on the left are unfathomable gulfs yawning for their destruction, and if it were not that divine grace made their feet as the hind's feet so that they are able to stand on high places, they would long ago have fallen to their eternal destruction.

False Assurance and Falling Away

Sadly, we have seen too many professors of Christianity fall away. It is true that when they have done so they have shown that they were not truly of us, for if they had been of us, they would have remained with us; but before they departed, they thought they were true believers, and the church thought they were as well. Some who seem most likely to be fruitful trees have turned out to be only cumberers of the ground (see Luke 13:7 KJV), bearing neither the fruit of the Spirit nor lasting evidence of a vital faith in Christ.

"How then can the Christian have any assurance of salvation?" the Arminian counters. "For if the people who fall away who surely believed before their defection from the faith that they were true Christians were never really so, on what grounds can any Christians know for certain that they are really saved? They may believe that they are true Christians, as those who fall away do, but how can they be certain that they have not deceived themselves and will not fall away from the faith as well?"

These questions raise an issue that pertains to professing Christians' state of mind; namely, the subjective assurance that they are Christians, which, because of the numerous grounds people resort to in their thinking—some appropriate, some quite inappropriate—as proofs that they are Christians can become extremely complex. Furthermore, these questions really should be a matter of concern for Arminian Christians as well as for Calvinist Christians, for they, too, must admit the possibility that people may believe they are Christians when, in fact, they are not.

In spite of the complexity of this issue, however, the Calvinist insists that certain propositions are still undeniably true. The first is there is such a thing as false assurance (which can undergird what we will call here *temporary faith*) that one is in the favor of God and the state of salvation (see WCF 18.1). And Calvinists would without hesitation insist that it is this false assurance these people have. But they would also insist that some vital fruit or evidence of genuine salvation was certainly missing from their "Christian experience" that put to the lie their assurance and, for the discerning, their profession as well. They themselves could most likely have discerned the missing fruit if they had examined themselves in the light of Scripture. For example, in Hebrews 6:1 the missing fruit is the total absence of growth in understanding even "the elementary principles of Christ"—a fruit that surely accompanies salvation (v. 9; see also 5:11–14), while in 2 Peter 2 the missing fruit is the complete absence in the false teachers of any holy religious affections. See Peter's characterization of them in verse 3 as covetous and deceptive and in verse 9 as unjust, to his charges in verse 10 that they follow "the lust of uncleanness and despise authority." In the following verses he writes that these slaves of corruption are bold, arrogant, and blasphemous; that they "carouse in the daytime" with "eyes full of adultery" (vv. 13, 14); that they "cannot cease from sin" (v. 14); and that they seek through their appeal to the lusts of the flesh to entice others to follow them.

True Assurance

Just as surely as Calvinists believe that people may entertain "false hopes and carnal presumptions" that they are in a state of salvation, Calvinists are equally persuaded that "such as truly believe in the Lord Jesus, and love Him in sincerity, endeavouring to walk in all good conscience before Him, may, in this life, be certainly assured that they are in the state of grace, and may rejoice in the hope of the glory of God, which hope shall never make them ashamed" (WCF 18.1). It is this certain assurance, they believe, that lies behind such biblical affirmations as the following:

> I am persuaded [*pepeismai*] that neither death nor life, nor angels nor principalities nor powers, nor things present nor things to come, nor height nor depth, nor any other created thing, shall be able to separate us from the love of God which is in Christ Jesus our Lord. (Rom. 8:38–39; see also the "we know [*oidamen*]" of v. 28)

> I know [*oida*] whom I have believed and am persuaded [*pepeismai*] that He is able to keep what I have committed to Him until that Day. (2 Tim. 1:12)

> By this we know [*ginōskomen*] that we know Him, if we keep His commandments. (1 John 2:3)

We know [*oidamen*] that we have passed from death to life, because we love the brethren. (1 John 3:14)

We know [*ginōskomen*] that we abide in Him, and He in us, because He has given us of His Spirit. (1 John 4:13)

These things I have written to you who believe in the name of the Son of God, that you may know [*eidēte*] that you have eternal life. (1 John 5:13)

It is the Christian's certain assurance of eternal glory that Augustus Toplady immortalizes in "A Debtor to Mercy Alone":

> A debtor to mercy alone,
> Of covenant mercy I sing;
> Nor fear, with Thy righteousness on,
> My person and off'ring to bring.
> The terrors of law and of God
> With me can have nothing to do;
> My Savior's obedience and blood
> Hide all my transgressions from view.
>
> The work which His goodness began,
> The arm of His strength will complete;
> His promise is yea and amen,
> And never was forfeited yet.
> Things future, nor things that are now,
> Nor all things below or above,
> Can make Him His purpose forgo,
> Or sever my soul from His love.
>
> My name from the palm of His hands
> Eternity will not erase;
> Impressed on His heart it remains,
> In marks of indelible grace.
> Yes, I to the end shall endure,
> As sure as the earnest is giv'n;
> More happy, but not more secure,
> The glorified spirits in heav'n.

Such assurance of salvation and of eternal life springs from (1) an intelligent understanding of the nature of salvation (2 Peter 1:2, 3, 5–6, 8; 3:18); (2) the recognition of the immutability of the gifts and calling of God (Rom. 11:29); (3) obedience to the commandments of God (1 John 2:3); (4) self-examination (2 Cor. 13:5); and (5) the inward witness of the Holy Spirit, who "Himself bears witness with our spirit that we are children of God" (Rom. 8:15–16; see also Gal. 4:6).

There can be no question but that it is the duty of every true Christian to cultivate such assurance through "the right use of ordinary means [of grace]" (WCF 18.3). Peter urges Christians to "be even more diligent to make your call and election sure" (2 Peter 1:10). But because of their immaturity in understanding the nature of their salvation; or inexcusable weakness of faith because they fail to cultivate it; or their disobedience to the commandments of God, their worldliness, their prayerlessness, or some other sin, some "true believers may have the assurance of their salvation divers ways shaken, diminished, and intermitted" (WCF 18.4). In other words, God will not permit true believers to persist in their immaturity or their sin and at the same time continue to enjoy unabated peace of conscience and joy in the Holy Spirit (see Pss. 32:4; 38:2; 51:12). He will chasten His true children (Heb. 12:6–8), and His hand of conviction will grow ever heavier on them. In the words of the Westminster Confession of Faith, they will "incur God's displeasure, …come to be deprived of some measure of their graces and comforts, …and bring temporal judgments upon themselves" (17.3). If they persist in their waywardness, God will even remove the light of His countenance from them and permit them to lose their assurance of salvation, which is surely the emotional state of mind lying behind David's cry, "Do not cast me away from Your presence, and do not take Your Holy Spirit from me" (Ps. 51:11). And He will not restore the light of His countenance to them "until they humble themselves, confess their sins, beg pardon, and renew their faith and repentance" (WCF 11.5). John Murray explains that even in their backslidden state,

> however weak may be the faith of a true believer, however severe
> may be his temptations, however perturbed his heart may be

respecting his own condition, he is never, as regards conscious-ness, in the condition that preceded the exercise of faith. The consciousness of the believer differs by a whole diameter from that of the unbeliever. At the lowest ebb of faith and hope and love his consciousness never drops to the level of the unbeliever at its highest pitch of confidence and assurance.[1]

To cite the words of the Westminster Confession once more in this regard: backslidden Christians are "never utterly destitute of that seed of God, and life of faith, that love of Christ and the brethren, that sincerity of heart, and conscience of duty, out of which, by the opera-tion of the Spirit, their assurance may, in due time, be revived; and by the which, in the mean time, they are supported from utter despair" (18.4). As He did with backslidden Peter, the Lord will continue to support His wayward children even while He chastens them when they fail to grow or when they fall into sin (Luke 22:31–32, 54–61; 24:34; see also Mark 16:7; John 21:15–19). But those who only out-wardly profess Christ but who are not truly saved will know neither the Spirit's inward witness, on the one hand, nor the Father's chasten-ing, on the other, but to the contrary will continue to ground whatever assurances they have that they are in a state of grace in false hopes and carnal presumptions that will perish.

Not to affirm the eternal security of the truly saved and actually to teach, as do Arminians, that those whom the Father elected, called, and justified and to whom He also freely gives, along with the gift of His Son, all things necessary to their salvation; to teach that those for whom the Son paid the penalty of sin by bearing their curse and dying their death, procuring thereby their salvation; and to teach that those whom the Holy Spirit has regenerated and sealed to the day of redemption can still finally lose their salvation and never be glorified because of some action on their part is truly an ill-advised counsel of despair. For in addition to the insult that such teaching hurls at the tri-une Godhead, it virtually places all Christians beyond the pale of final salvation since it makes their attainment of it turn ultimately on their own vacillating human will and efforts as they seek to keep themselves

---

1. John Murray, "The Assurance of Faith," in *Collected Writings*, 2:265.

in the faith. But no Christians are capable of keeping themselves in the state of salvation through sheer force of will.

To all of us who are conscious of spiritual perils and fearful lest we should be overcome by them, the doctrine of the final perseverance of the saints affords the richest encouragement. If the Holy Spirit will help me to set forth this doctrine so as to commend its truth to your understanding, I will be glad of heart because the truth will make you glad and strong and thankful. Without further comment I will first expound the apostle's words in order to show in some detail the reason for his confidence; he writes, "Being confident of this very thing" (Phil. 1:6); second, I will support his confidence in the final perseverance of the saints by setting forth additional grounds for the doctrine; and third, I will draw out some uses from this doctrine for our spiritual benefit.

The Apostle's Words

He speaks of the "good work" (Phil. 1:6), which I must remind you will often be a painful and lengthy work, that God had begun in the hearts of "all the saints in Christ Jesus who are in Philippi" (v. 1). This is obviously the good work of salvation, for to bring people from darkness into light is good, and to deliver them from the bondage of their natural corruption and to make them the Lord's free people is clearly a good work. It is good for them, it is good for society, it is good for the church of God, and it is good for the glory of God Himself. It is so good a work that the one who receives it becomes the heir of all good as well as the advocate and author of further good here. This good work is the best that a person can receive. To make a person healthy in body and wealthy in estate, to educate his or her mind and to train his or her faculties are good, but in comparison with the salvation of the soul they all sink into insignificance. The work of sanctification is a good work in the highest possible sense since it influences people by good motives, sets them toward good works, introduces them to other good people of like good works, gives them fellowship with the good angels of heaven, and in the end makes them like God Himself.

This is also a good work because it originates in the goodness of God. As it is always good to show mercy, so it is preeminently good on God's part to work on sinful people so as to renew them again after His image. This work of grace is rooted in the divine goodness of the Father, wrought by the self-denying goodness of the Son, and is daily watered by the life-giving goodness of the Holy Spirit. It springs from good and leads to good, so it is altogether good.

The apostle calls it a good *work*, and in the deepest sense it is indeed a miraculous work to convert a soul. If Niagara Falls could suddenly be made to flow upward instead of dashing downward, it would not be as great a miracle as the changing of a perverse will and the raging passions of sinful people. To remove the leopard's spots is difficult, but it is only a surface work. To renew the very core of a person and tear sin from its hold on the human heart is not only the finger of God; it is God baring His holy arm. This is because conversion is the equivalent of God's making a new world, for Paul tells us that we are new creations (2 Cor. 5:17). It is a work that has no parallel. It is beyond making water flow uphill. It is unique and unrivaled, seeing that the entire Godhead must cooperate in it. To implant the new nature in a Christian requires the decree of the eternal Father, the death of the ever-blessed Son, and the fullness of the operation of the adorable Spirit. Yes, it is a divine *work* indeed.

Now note that Paul affirms that this work was *begun* by God. Quite evidently the apostle was not a believer in the remarkable powers that some theologians ascribe to free will, the modern Diana of the Ephesians. He declared that this good work was begun by God, which means that the faintest desire that ultimately blossoms into the fragrant flower of earnest prayer and humble faith that leads to salvation is the work of God. No, you were never beforehand with the Lord; He was always beforehand with your soul. The first step toward ending the separation between God and you was taken by the Father. It will never happen that the corrupt nature will educe from itself the germ of the new life or sigh after holiness and God. It simply is not so; it is a lie from top to bottom. No grain or vestige of spiritual good lies within the hearts of unregenerate people. They are aliens, insensible, dead to all good; and they cannot be restored to God except by an agency that is altogether outside them and from above. If you could fully develop what is in the heart of man you would produce a devil, for that is the spirit that works in the sons of disobedience. The fact is that spiritual life has departed from the natural man; he is dead in sin, and life must come to him from the Giver of life, or he will remain dead forever. The work that is in the soul of true Christians did not begin with them; it was begun by the Lord.

Paul also affirms that the good work that God began *He must carry on.* Either God must perform it, or it will not get done. Along the road to heaven, from first leaving the swine trough to joyfully entering the banquet hall of heaven, we must be enabled to take every step by divine grace. If my finger were on the golden latch of paradise and my foot were on its threshold, I could not take the last step to enter heaven unless the grace that had brought me safe thus far should enable me to complete my pilgrimage. Salvation is God's work, not man's. This is the theology that Jonah learned in the Great Fish College in the University of the Great Deep, and it would be a good thing if many of our divines in these days could be sent there, for their learning often puffs them up with the idea of human sufficiency. But those who are schooled and disciplined in the college of Jonah's deep experience and have learned about the vileness of their own heart as they peer into its chambers of imagery will confess that, from first to last, salvation is "not of him who wills, nor of him who runs, but of God who shows mercy" (Rom. 9:16).

The apostle stresses still further that this work, once begun, *most certainly will be carried out.* Observe that he declares that he was confident of this truth. And why? When a person commences a work and leaves it half completed, it is most likely from want of power, want of foresight, want of ability, or want of wherewithal. But can the omnipotent, all-wise God cease from a work because of an unseen difficulty that He is not able to overcome? He sees the end from the beginning. He is almighty. His arm is not shortened so that it cannot save. Nothing is too hard for Him. So it is a base reflection on the wisdom and power of God to believe that He will ever begin a work that He will not in due time conduct to a happy and fruitful conclusion.

God did not begin the work in any person's soul without due deliberation and counsel with Himself. From all eternity He knew the circumstances in which He would place that person. He saw the hardness of the human heart and the fickleness of human love. If then He deemed it wise to begin to redeem that person, how can one suppose that He will change or amend His resolve? There is no conceivable reason for God to cease His work. Show me the world that He abandoned and threw aside half formed. I will challenge you on lower ground: point out to me a plant that has about it a semblance of incompleteness. As for all that people complete, let them polish it as much as they want, the microscope reveals it is but roughly finished. But all God's works are finished to perfection with wondrous care. And yet, though this is true everywhere else, some foolish preachers want to persuade us that this great work of salvation of the soul may be begun by God but He may desert it and leave it incomplete and there will be spirits lost forever on whom the Holy Spirit once exerted His sanctifying power, for whom the blessed Redeemer shed His precious blood and on whom the eternal Father once looked with eyes of complacent joy. It is a miserable doctrine that says saints may lose their salvation, that the sheep may be rent by the wolves, that the stones in the walls of the spiritual temple may yet be scattered to the four winds, that the members of Christ may be rent from his sacred body, and that the spouse of Christ may be mutilated. I believe in the final perseverance of every person in whom the regenerating grace of God has wrought a change of nature. Those who have been born of God cannot die; if the living seed is in them, the devil cannot destroy it.

In nothing does the Lord turn aside from his intent. Has He spoken it, and will He not do it? Has He purposed, and will it not come to pass (Isa. 46:11)? There is a world of sound argument in the quiet words the apostle uses for the perseverance of the saints. We can be sure that He who made the tear to flow will wipe away every tear from the same eye. He who brought us to the cross will bring us to the crown. He who made us look on Him whom we pierced and to mourn because of Him will cause us to see the King in His beauty in the land that is fairer than day. This is the truth that the text quite plainly teaches us.

> Each object of God's love is sure
> to reach the heavenly goal;

for neither sin nor Satan can
destroy the blood-washed soul.

Satan may vex, and unbelief
the saved one may annoy,
but he must conquer; yes, as sure
as Jesus reigns in joy.

The precious blood of God's dear Son
shall ne'er be spilt in vain;
the soul on Christ believing,
with Christ forever reign!

Grounds for Paul's Confidence

The first ground is the *express teaching of Holy Scripture* in this text and elsewhere in Scripture, which is saturated with this truth; the few verses or passages alleged to teach the contrary have been many times explained by insightful exegetes. Consider the following passages:[2]

The righteous will hold to his way, and he who has clean hands will be stronger and stronger. (Job 17:9)

I am continually with You;
You [Lord] hold me by my right hand.
You will guide me with Your counsel,
And afterward receive me to glory. (Ps. 73:23–24)

I [Jesus] give [my sheep] eternal life, and they shall never perish; neither shall anyone snatch them out of My hand. My Father, who has given them to Me, is greater than all; and no one is able to snatch them out of My Father's hand. (John 10:28–29)

I am persuaded that neither death nor life, nor angels nor principalities nor powers, nor things present nor things to come, nor height nor depth, nor any other created thing, shall be able to separate us from the love of God which is in Christ Jesus our Lord. (Rom. 8:38–39)

---

2. See also Pss. 37:23–24; 125:1–2; John 6:38–39; 17:11–12; Rom. 11:29.

[Our Lord Jesus Christ] will also confirm you to the end, that you may be blameless in the day of our Lord Jesus Christ. (1 Cor. 1:8)

God, determining to show more abundantly to the heirs of promise the immutability of His counsel, confirmed it by an oath, that by two immutable things, in which it is impossible for God to lie, we might have strong consolation, who have fled for refuge to lay hold of the hope set before us.

This hope we have as an anchor of the soul, both sure and steadfast. (Heb. 6:17–19)

[We] are kept by the power of God through faith for salvation ready to be revealed in the last time. (1 Peter 1:5)

Second, in addition to the express testimony of Scripture, this doctrine is supported by *all the attributes of God*, and if those who have believed in Christ can be finally lost, then all the attributes of God are in peril. Where is His wisdom if He began a work that He did not intend to finish? Where is His power if the obstinacy of people's sin is greater than His grace? Where is His immutability if He casts away those whom He once loved? Where is His faithfulness to His promises that He has sealed with His unchangeable covenant and His oath? Where is His grace if He casts away those who trust Him, if after having tantalized us with sips of love He will not bring us to drink finally and fully from the fountainhead? Where is His veracity if he leaves the soul who has looked to Him for His mercy and is then finally lost?

Third, what kind of *atonement* did Jesus accomplish if those for whom He died can finally perish? His atonement obviously did not save them if they finally perish, and if He did not do for others what He did not do for them, then His death saved no one, which is blasphemous to suggest. The Scriptures teach, however, that Jesus Christ rendered to divine justice full satisfaction for the sins of His people. Since this is so, how can the child of God whose sins were laid on Christ be cast into hell? In the name of everlasting justice, how can a person whose guilt was borne by Christ also be regarded as guilty unless God unjustly enacts double jeopardy and sacrifices His honor in doing so? Those who have trusted Christ must surely be brought to glory because Christ's atonement requires it. Which is also to say, to cite Charles Haddon Spurgeon, "Christ so died that he infallibly secured the salvation [of His people]…, who through Christ's death not only may be saved but are saved, must be saved, and cannot by any possibility run the hazard of being anything but saved."[3]

Fourth, the *doctrine of justification* demands it. All people who believe in Christ have been justified freely from all things from which they could not have been justified by the law of Moses. They are free of all accusations. The holy boast of the apostle ought to be like rolling thunder in your ears: "Who shall bring a charge against God's elect? It is God who justifies" (Rom. 8:33). If nothing can be laid to the charge of God's elect, if no one can accuse them, then who will condemn them? Certainly not the Father; it is He who justifies. Certainly not the Son; it is He who died and rose again for us.

Fifth is the *intercession of Christ* for His own in heaven. "He is also able to save to the uttermost those who come to God through Him, since He always lives to make intercession for them" (Heb. 7:25).

Sixth, every believer is *a member of Christ's body*. What imagination is so depraved that it can picture Christ, the Head, united to a body in which the members frequently decay—hand and foot, arm and leg, eye and ear—rotting off so as to require fresh members to take their place, with the prospect that Christ could eternally wind up an amputee? Such an image is atrocious!

Seventh, the *nature of the inner life of Christians* guarantees that they will not go back forever to the old life. Consider the following passages. In the gospel of John, Jesus says, "Whoever drinks of the water that I shall give him will never thirst. But the water that I shall give him will become in him a fountain of water springing up into everlasting life" (4:14). Will anyone say that the water Jesus gives His people perhaps will dry up and cease to flow? In a second passage in John, Jesus declares,

> "He who believes in Me has everlasting life. I am the bread of life."…
> "He who eats this bread will live forever." (6:47–48, 58)

---

3. C. H. Spurgeon, Sermon #181, "Particular Redemption," in *C. H. Spurgeon's Sermons: The New Park Street Pulpit* (Grand Rapids: Reformation Heritage Books, 2024), 4:135.

In 1 Peter 1:23, the apostle writes that we have "been born again, not of corruptible seed but incorruptible, through the word of God which lives and abides forever." If this seed is incorruptible, how can anyone say that the righteous can become corrupt and fall from grace? Finally, in Colossians 3:3 Paul writes, "For you died, and your life is hidden with Christ in God." The life that Jesus implants in the hearts of His people is allied to His life, which means that God Himself would die if a Christian were to be lost since the life that has been given to the Christian is the life of God Himself.

The Westminster Larger Catechism, question 79, summarizes all this: "True believers, by reason of the unchangeable love of God, and his decree and covenant to give them perseverance, their inseparable union with Christ, his continual intercession for them, and the Spirit and the seed of God abiding in them, can neither totally nor finally fall away from the state of grace, but are kept by the power of God through faith unto salvation."

I will leave the doctrine for your meditation, and I pray that the Holy Spirit will put this teaching beyond doubt in your souls. But remember what the doctrine is: the Bible does not teach that all who believe in Christ will be saved regardless of how they live. It teaches that all who believe in Christ receive the Holy Spirit, who will lead them in the way of holiness from strength to strength until they come to the perfection that God will work in them at the coming of His own dear Son.

Useful Inferences from This Doctrine

The first inference is obvious: there is much in this great biblical truth by way of comfort for you who are the children of God. You know that God some time ago revealed Himself to you savingly. You can remember times when your walk with God was peculiarly precious. You were certain of Christ's love, and you loved Him. Now, if some temporary depression of spirit has overwhelmed you, remember His words: "I am the LORD, I do not change" (Mal. 3:6). You may change, but He does not. Should He seem to be hiding His face from you, you can believe that He still loves you. Do not judge Him by outward providences; judge Him by the teaching of His Word.

> Determin'd to save,
> He watch'd o'er my path,
> When, Satan's blind slave,
> I sported with death;
> And can He have taught me
> To trust in His name,
> And thus far have brought me,
> To put me to shame?[4]

Never, no never, will He ever leave you or forsake you.

The teaching of the perseverance of the saints, second, should also suggest to Christians the need for constant diligence to walk in holiness that they may persevere to the end. "What?" exclaims someone. "I would have thought the very reverse, for if the believer is ever safe, what is the need for diligence?"

My reply is this: You misunderstand the doctrine. If God is to keep a person *in* holiness until life's end, surely there is a need *for* holiness, and the doctrine that the believer shall be so kept in holiness is one of the best means of producing the desired result. If any of you could somehow be infallibly assured that in a certain line of work you would make a vast amount of money, would that confidence lead you to lie in bed all day? No, the assurance that you would prosper would make you diligent to pursue that business with might and main. Just as the certainty of a thing does not hinder people from striving after it but rather quickens them, even so the belief that we shall one day be perfect never hinders the true believer from diligence but becomes the highest incentive to make a person struggle against the corruptions of the flesh and to seek to persevere according to God's promise.

"Well," asks someone, "if God guarantees final perseverance, why do I need to pray to be kept forever?" How could one pray for perseverance if God had not guaranteed it? I dare not pray for what God has not promised, but as soon as it is promised, I know that I can pray for it. And when I see it in the Bible, I labor for it.

---

4. John Newton, "Begone Unbelief," in *Olney Hymns* (London: James Duncan, 1825), book 3, hymn 37 (247).

"Say what you will," says another, "you are inconsistent." I am responsible to address as best I can your questions, but I am not bound to give you understanding if you have none. It is hard trying to make things appear right to eyes that squint. And it often happens that people cannot see truth because they do not want to see it. But the practical effect of this doctrine is my main point here: those who believe they can fall from grace run awful risks and constantly live in fear of falling, and they do in fact fall—a thousand times a day they fall!—while those of us who believe that we cannot fall if we have truly believed walk with all carefulness and circumspection and live with joy in that walk. I live as if my salvation depended wholly on me, all the while relying on my Lord, knowing that it does not depend on me in any sense at all. We Calvinists live as the Arminian doctrine is supposed to make people live—which is exactly as the Calvinistic doctrine actually does make people live—that is, with true holiness and joy, with earnestness of purpose, and with gratitude toward God, who has secured our salvation through Jesus Christ our Lord.

We may also learn from Philippians 1:6, third, how to persevere. The apostle's reason for believing that the Philippians would persevere was not because they were good and earnest people but because God had begun His good work in them. Therefore, our ground for holding to the narrow way is our constant confidence in God's work. The moment you think you have fallen, trust God. Just say, "Lord, I am a sinner, and You died for sinners, and I will cling to that. Lord, I believe today if I never believed before." Fall from grace? Why, it is nonsense! This is the true doctrine of perseverance: it is to persevere in recognizing that you are nothing and letting Christ be your all. It is to persevere in resting wholly and solely in Christ and in the keeping power of His grace.

Does not this grand doctrine of our biblical and Reformed faith attract you? We preach no rickety gospel that will not bear your weight. It is not like a car whose axle may break or whose wheels may come off. The everlasting God who wrote His law on your hearts has pledged Himself by covenant and by oath—by two immutable things in which He cannot lie—that He will not let you depart from Him. He will keep you, and He will not let you wander back into sin and be finally lost, and if even for a time you should stray, He will restore you again to the path of righteousness. So cast your lot with Christ. When you trusted Christ, His precious promise to keep you forever became yours.

Study Questions

1. What images does this chapter use to communicate that the perseverance of the saints all the way to glory is a spiritual miracle?

2. How should we respond to the falling away of people who profess to be Christians?

3. What affirmations of the Holy Scriptures show us that assurance of salvation is possible?

4. What is the basis of assurance?

5. What duty do believers have with respect to assurance? What will happen if a believer neglects this duty and backslides?

6. Why is it an insult to each person of the Trinity to teach that the truly saved can lose their salvation?

7. What does Paul teach about God's work of salvation in Philippians 1:6?

8. How do the express teachings of Holy Scripture give confidence in the perseverance of the saints?

9. What other grounds are there for confidence in the true Christian's perseverance?

10. How should this doctrine be applied for (1) comfort, (2) diligence, and (3) trust?

CHAPTER 10

Glorification

The Spirit Himself bears witness with our spirit that we are children of God, and if children, then heirs—heirs of God and joint heirs with Christ.
—ROMANS 8:16–17

He [will] make known the riches of His glory on the vessels of mercy, which He had prepared beforehand for glory.
—ROMANS 9:23

God…[has] called us to His eternal glory by Christ Jesus.
—1 PETER 5:10

In Romans 9:23, Paul writes of our being God's heirs and of the *"riches of His glory"* that the Father will someday make fully known to us, and Peter tells us that the God of all grace has *"called* us to *His eternal glory* by Christ Jesus" (1 Peter 5:10).

Called—that is where your individual salvation began: called to repentance unto life; called to continual confession of sin; called to continual faith in Jesus Christ; called to conversion; called to renewal and consecration; called to pardon and justification; called to adoption; called to sanctification, both definitive and processive; called to dying more and more to sin and living more and more to righteousness; called to perseverance in faith, hope, and love; and here called to eternal glory.

God's eternal glory—that is where it will conclude, with the glory of purified character; the glory of perfected humanity; the glory of complete victory over all our enemies, including death, our last enemy; the glory of divine approval; the glory of rare wisdom and knowledge; the glory of immense riches beyond all manner of magnificence and splendor; the glory that will make us famous, for we "shall shine…like the stars forever and ever" (Dan. 12:3); the glory that will singularly honor us, for we will be a special people, a royal priesthood, a race of beings lifted up to reveal our Maker's character above and beyond all the rest of His works; the glory of reflecting the glory of God in the unsearchable riches of His grace; the glory of being connected with Jesus in everything; the glory of dwelling immediately in the presence of God; the glory that will never end; the glory that will be His eternal glory.

The word *glory* has the idea of weight, which Paul hints at when he speaks of the "weight of glory" (2 Cor. 4:17). God's glory is the only glory that has any weight about it. God's glory is solid, true, and real, and the one who gets it possesses no mere name or dream or tinsel but that which will withstand the fires of judgment and remain throughout all the ages. All else is as light as a feather. Take all the glories of this world and combine them, and they are outweighed by the small dust on the balance by God's rich, eternal glory. Place them here in the hollow of my hand, all of them; a child may blow them away like the wispy seedlings of the dandelion.

How can I describe the glory of God? I will set before you a strange scriptural picture. In Esther 6 King Ahasuerus decreed that a singular honor should be paid to a certain subject in his kingdom, Mordecai, because of his fidelity to his king. But what honor? Mordecai's enemy Haman, thinking he was the individual to be honored, suggested this:

> "For the man whom the king delights to honor, let a royal robe be brought which the king has worn, and a horse on which the king has ridden, which has a royal crest placed on its head. Then let this robe and horse be delivered to the hand of one of the king's most noble princes, that he may array the man whom the king delights to honor. Then parade him on horseback through the city square, and proclaim before him: 'Thus shall it be done to the man whom the king delights to honor!'"

Then the king said to Haman, "Hurry, take the robe and the horse, as you have suggested, and do so for Mordecai the Jew…. Leave nothing undone of all that you have spoken."

So Haman took the robe and the horse, arrayed Mordecai and led him on horseback through the city square, and proclaimed before him, "Thus shall it be done to the man whom the king delights to honor!" (vv. 7–11)

Can you imagine Mordecai's surprise when the king's robe was put on him and when he found himself placed on the king's horse with his enemy beneath him? This can serve as a picture, but admittedly a very poor one, of what will happen to us. We will be glorified with the glory of God. The best robe of Christ's perfect righteousness, the finest of heaven's array, will be placed on us; all our enemies will be beneath our feet; and we will be paraded before all the heavenly host for them to behold our eternal glory.

I would love to be able to tell you everything about this glory that will be ours, but that would mean a limitation of the infinite glory of God that is beyond anyone's knowing except for God Himself, so I confess that at best I will lisp and stammer as I proceed. You may recall that Paul saw a little of it for a short time, and he confessed that he heard things that it is not lawful for a man to utter, and I do not doubt that he felt totally at a loss for words when it came to describing even to himself what he had seen (see 2 Cor. 12:2–4). Though he was a master of language, for once he was overpowered; the grandeur of his theme silenced him.

So what can we do in that arena where even Paul's talents broke down? Our eyes too have seen wonderful things—glorious sunrises and sunsets, breathtaking Alpine heights and ocean marvels—that, once seen, cling to our memories throughout life. Yet nature even at its best cannot give us an idea of the supernatural glory that God has prepared for His people. Our ears have heard sweet harmonies and gorgeous melodies in Handel's *Messiah* and Mendelssohn's *Elijah*, and we have listened to speeches that thrilled us. But no melody of symphonic instruments or charm of oratory can ever raise us to a conception of the eternal glory that God has laid up for those who love Him. Poets have woven in the looms of their fancy fair descriptions of our final destiny that have made our minds sparkle with their beauty and brightness. Their imaginations have reveled and rioted in their fantastic creations, roaming among mountains of gold and swimming in oceans of wine and rivers of milk and have made us long to see what Paul saw and more. I am thinking now of "The Sands of Time Are Sinking" by Samuel Rutherford:

> The King there in His beauty
> Without a veil is seen;
> It were a well-spent journey,
> Though sev'n deaths lay between:
> The Lamb with His fair army
> Doth on Mount Zion stand,
> And glory, glory dwelleth
> In Emmanuel's land.

In the twelfth century, Bernard of Cluny acknowledged in "Jerusalem the Golden" that thoughts failed him when he tried to visualize our future glory:

> Jerusalem the golden, with milk and honey blest—
> The sight of it refreshes the weary and oppressed.
> I know not, oh, I know not what joys await us there,
> What radiancy of glory, what bliss beyond compare:
> To sing the hymn unending with all the martyr throng,
> Amidst the halls of Zion resounding full with song.
>
> They stand, those halls of Zion, all jubilant with song,
> And bright with many an angel, and all the martyr throng.
> The Prince is ever in them, the daylight is serene;
> The pastures of the blessed are blessed in glorious sheen.

Such words inspire us, but the poets' imaginations and words have never been able to open the gates of heaven—even an inch—to us. But let us try to say what we can, based on Scripture, first, about the nature of our future glorification.

The Nature of Our Future Glorification

Our individual salvation encompasses not only all three tenses of time—we *have been saved* from the guilt and condemnation of sin by our justification, *are being saved* from the power of sin by our sanctification, and *will be completely saved* someday from the very presence of sin by our glorification—but also the whole person, body and soul. God will not be satisfied with His saving work in our behalf until we stand before Him as saved people in Christ, redeemed both in spirit and in body, nor will our great salvation be consummated until He has brought our full and final glorification to reality. Consequently, while there is a sense in which death itself now serves the Christian, in that "the souls of believers are at their death made perfect in holiness, and do immediately pass into glory," it is nonetheless true that "their bodies, being still united to Christ, do rest in their graves till the resurrection" (WSC 37). In other words, while the intermediate state of believers in heaven, brought to pass in God's will when He calls His children to Himself through death, is a more blessed state than this present one, it is not the best and most glorious state. Accordingly, death is not the ultimate experience to which Christians should longingly look. I never counsel dying people to look to death as their hope. Rather, I tell them that their blessed hope is the glorious appearing (or the appearing of the glory) of their great God and Savior Jesus Christ (Titus 2:13), at whose coming those who have died in the faith and those who are alive at the time of His coming

> shall all be changed—in a moment, in the twinkling of an eye, at the last trumpet. For the trumpet will sound, and the dead will be raised incorruptible, and we shall be changed. For this corruptible must put on incorruption, and this mortal must put on immortality. So when this corruptible has put on incorruption, and this mortal has put on immortality, then shall be brought to pass the saying that is written:
>
> "Death is swallowed up in victory."
>> "O Death, where is your sting?
>> O Hades, where is your victory?"

> The sting of death is sin, and the strength of sin is the law. But thanks be to God, who gives us the victory through our Lord Jesus Christ. (1 Cor. 15:51–57)

"At the resurrection, believers, being raised up in glory, shall be openly acknowledged, and acquitted in the day of judgment, and made perfectly blessed in the full enjoying of God to all eternity" (WSC 38). All the more will their state of blessedness, as the consequence of their full and open acquittal in the judgment, be evident by its contrast to the state of those "vessels of wrath prepared for destruction, and that [God] might make known *the riches of His glory* on the vessels of mercy, which He had prepared beforehand for glory" (Rom. 9:22–23). For whereas they will enter into everlasting life and receive the fullness of joy and refreshing that shall come from the presence of the Lord, the wicked who do not know God and do not obey the gospel of our Lord Jesus Christ will receive the penalty of eternal destruction away from the approving presence of the Lord and from the glory of His power.

At this point we will enter our glorified state, both the goal toward which the triune Godhead, in all of their salvific exercises, have been relentlessly driving from the moment of creation, and the ultimate end that was the first of the decrees in the eternal plan of salvation. Our final glorification will mean something for creation, for us, and for Christ. Let us think about what our glorification will mean for these subjects.

The Meaning of Our Glorification for Creation

With the arrival of our full adoption as sons through the redemption of our bodies at the resurrection (Rom. 8:23), and not till then, the renewal of creation itself will occur. Creation will be "delivered from the bondage of corruption into the glorious liberty of the children of God" (v. 21; see also vv. 19–20). Peter describes the world that will then be—the fulfillment of Isaiah 65:17 and 66:22—as "new heavens and a new earth in which righteousness dwells" (2 Peter 3:13). John declares that in the new heavens and new earth, "there shall be no more death, nor sorrow, nor crying.... For the former things have passed away" (Rev. 21:4). Biblical scholars have ardently debated whether the new heavens and new earth involve simply the renewal of the present universe or a complete destruction followed by re-creation ex nihilo. The preponderance of evidence suggests a renewal, but the transformation of the universe will be so complete that, for all intents and purposes, it will introduce a radically new order of existence for the heavens and the earth.

The Meaning of Our Glorification for Christians

In our glorified state we believers, having received the fullness of our adoption by the resurrection of our bodies from the dead (Rom. 8:23), will be fully and finally conformed to the likeness of the Son of God. For at His coming, the Lord Jesus Christ "will transform our lowly body that it may be conformed to His glorious body, according to the working by which He is able even to subdue all things to Himself" (Phil. 3:21). Moreover, we will then reflect the holy character of our Savior (Rom. 8:29), our wills being "made perfectly and immutably free to do good alone, in the state of glory" (WCF 9.5). This is the highest end conceivable for created beings not only by men but also by God Himself, who could not contemplate or determine a higher destiny for His creatures. With trenchant insight John Murray observes that though Christ will be the *firstborn* at that time, a term referring to priority and supereminence, His will be a

> supereminence among brethren, and therefore the supereminence involved has no meaning except in that relation [to His brethren]. Hence, though there can be no underestimation of the preeminence belonging to the Son as the first begotten, yet the interdependence is just as necessary. The glory bestowed upon the redeemed is derived from the relation they sustain to the "firstborn." But the specific character involved in being the "firstborn" is derived from the relation he sustains to the redeemed in that capacity. Hence they must be glorified together.[1]

It is little wonder, then, that Paul can inform Christians, who were originally called "for the obtaining of the glory of our Lord Jesus Christ" (2 Thess. 2:14) and who will "be glorified together" with Christ

---

1. John Murray, "The Goal of Sanctification," in *Collected Writings*, 2:315.

(Rom. 8:17), "that the sufferings of this present time are not worthy to be compared with the glory which shall be revealed in us" (v. 18)—indeed, that "our light affliction, which is but for a moment, is working for us a far more exceeding and eternal weight of glory" (2 Cor. 4:17).

We will then understand better what it means to be heirs of God and joint heirs with Jesus Christ. We know some things now. This short statement is one that none of us can fully comprehend, but I can give you some of the Bible's descriptions of our inheritance.

In Matthew 25:34, Jesus teaches that our inheritance is "the kingdom prepared for you from the foundation of the world." In 1 Corinthians 3:21–22 Paul declares, "All things are yours: whether… the world or life or death, or things present or things to come—all are yours." The richest man who ever lived could not say that, but the poorest Christian who ever lived can. Then, in Titus 3:7, he calls us "heirs according to the hope of eternal life." The writer to the Hebrews says we are those who will "inherit salvation" (1:14) and who are "the heirs of promise" (6:17). James 2:5 declares that we are "heirs of the kingdom which He promised to those who love Him." First Peter 1:4 describes our inheritance as "incorruptible and undefiled and that does not fade away, reserved in heaven for you" and later adds that we are "heirs together of the grace of life" (3:7). And Revelation 21:7 tells us, "He who overcomes shall inherit all things."

What does all this mean? It means that we are heirs of every spiritual blessing in heaven! Think about what God has promised us. Here, the most vivid imagination must stretch its wings and the most capacious thoughts must fly abroad, and when they have crossed the remotest bounds of space, they have only just commenced their endless journey to comprehend our inheritance that is beyond our finite knowing.

Paul speaks of Christ as God's "indescribable gift" to us (2 Cor. 9:15). But even this thought, as great as it is, is only part of our inheritance, for to be heirs of God means that God Himself belongs to us. David declared in Psalms 16:5–6 and 142:5 and Asaph did in Psalm 73:26 that the Lord is the portion of their inheritance. You have inherited God! You are His portion; He is your portion. You have God's power to protect you, His truth to guide you, His justice to defend you, His immutability to safeguard you, His promises to reassure you, His infinity to enrich you, His heart to love you, access to His throne to comfort you, and His glory to cover you. And you have all these things forever.

How often the statement "You are *my* God" occurs in the Psalms! But that statement could never be the utterance of any mere human—not a David, not a Paul, not the greatest saint—had it not been first in God's eternal purpose on the lips of Christ in that awful hour when He cried, "My God, My God, why have You forsaken Me?" (Matt. 27:46; Mark 15:34). So when you frame those words "my God" on your lips as a description of your inheritance, know that it was Jesus's "My God" on the cross that enabled you to put them there and to become an heir of God. Know that every aspect of your inheritance is bloodstained with the royal blood of the Son of God.

According to Hebrews 4:16 you have free access to your Father's throne of grace at all times, in midnight's darkest hour, in noontide's brightest heat. Whatever your desires, your difficulties, your trials, your wants, you are at liberty to spread them all before Him. It doesn't matter what your needs may be, for there is fullness of supply in Christ, and it is there for you. All this suggests that in at least some respects God is as much our God as He is Christ's God and as much our Father as He is Christ's Father. Of course, God is Christ's God by nature; He is our God by adoption. But adopted children are still fully children. It is the partnership of the claimants to this inheritance. We are informed that we who are God's children are not only heirs of God but also joint heirs with Christ.

Joint Heirs with Christ

This feature of our inheritance provides us, first, with *the test of our heirship*. None of us are an heir of God alone; we cannot be. We can be an heir of God only through being in company with Christ. Are you and Christ in company together, or do you stand alone? If you stand alone, you are a poor, miserable, bankrupt sinner. So do not stand alone; you will perish if you do. Have you trusted Christ? Do you live for Christ? Do you approach the throne of grace through Christ? Is Christ your Lord, your Savior, your elder brother, your friend? This is the test of your heirship. If you are an heir of God, it is because you are in Christ. If you are not in Christ, you are not in the family of God and not an heir of God at all. You who are "without Christ," the apostle Paul declares, are "without God," and of all the terrible places in which to be without Him, you are without God in this present evil world (Eph. 2:12).

While this feature of our inheritance is the test of our heirship, it is, second, *the sweetest part of all our inheritance.* If I know that I am one with Christ and a fellow heir with Him, it is like heaven here on earth to my soul. Indeed, I will love heaven someday all the more and love all that God will give me by and by all the better because Christ and I together are going to share the inheritance. Now, wherever Christ is, it is good to be and to go shares with Him. It makes everything sweeter to be able to enjoy His company and your time with Him. When our Lord prayed in His High Priestly Prayer, "Father, I desire that they also whom You gave Me may be with Me where I am, that they may behold My glory" (John 17:24), He knew that His people would prize something that belonged to Him better than anything else in all the world, or even in heaven itself. This is the sweetest part of our inheritance—that it is a joint heirship with Christ.

Our joint heirship with Christ also shows *the greatness of our inheritance* because if we are coheirs, it cannot be a little thing that we are to share with Him. He owns this universe—every star, every planet, this entire globe, all the cattle on a thousand hills, every square inch of it. All belongs to Him! Now because of the travail of His soul in my behalf, I would have Him crowned with many crowns and have Him occupy the highest place of honor in heaven and have Him receive the highest honors heaven can afford. So if I would desire these things for Him, can you even begin to imagine what the Father is going to give Him as the reward for His atoning work? What must the greatness of the Father's infinite largess be that He will bestow on His well-beloved Son for His obedience? Follow that line of thought as far as you can—it will finally overwhelm you—and then remember that you are a joint heir with Christ in all that the Father will give Him. What He has, He is going to share with you.

This joint heirship also is *the guarantee of our inheritance*. Multitudes of people have been ruined financially by buying shares in companies that seemed to be sound, only to find that their financial officers were corrupt and their paper worth but a few pennies on the dollar. But one need not mind going shares if one has nothing at all and the other partner is the wealthiest person in the whole universe. Just so, what a blessing it is to be a joint heir with Christ because we bring to the partnership nothing, and He who is King of kings and Lord of lords cannot fail to inherit all that His Father has promised Him. How secure, then, is the inheritance of the saints!

I will conclude this point by observing that our joint heirship with Christ *insures His love to us*. And since this is so, should it not also bind our hearts to Him? If we are to share in His glorious inheritance there, should we not gladly share in His shame here? Does someone want to speak an evil word against Him? Then let that word fall on us as well. If we are to be with Him there and share in His glory, it is only right that we should be willing here to bear His reproach and to share the dishonor of His cross as far as we are able to do so, for we are joint heirs with Him, partners, if you will, in the same company.

What Jesus Desires

In our Lord's High Priestly Prayer in John 17, three times he requested (*erōtaō*; vv. 9, 15), but in verse 24 he used a stronger word (*thelō*); He said, "Father, I desire." I would not force this word so as to make it a command, for the Savior does not speak this way to the Father, but it still has a more elevated quality about it than asking. Our Lord here speaks as the Son of God who is Himself God; He addresses the great and holy Father as one equal with Him, and He exercises the prerogative of His eternal Sonship. He says, "I desire." And He petitioned His Father that those whom the Father gave Him "may be with Me where I am, that they may behold My glory which You have given Me."

I do not wonder that Jesus wants His brothers and sisters to be with Him for this purpose since love always pines for a partner in its joys. It is an instinct of affection to seek fellowship in joy. The Lord Jesus is truly human, and He feels the unselfish desire of the loving human heart. Our Lord is desirous that we should participate in His glory. He knows that nothing will be a greater joy for us than to see Him exalted; therefore, He would give us this highest form of delight. It is joy to Jesus to let us behold His joy, and it will be glory to us to behold His glory. And by His prayer He willed for us heaven's *highest joy*, its *sweetest employment*, and its *greatest privilege*. Let us consider each of these in turn.

The first is that which is heaven's *highest joy*: "Father, I desire that they also whom You gave Me may *be with Me where I am*" (John 17:24). Notice that every word in the sentence is necessary to its fullness. He does not say, "I desire that they also whom You gave Me may be where I am," but rather "may be *with Me* where I am." And He desires not only that they be with Him but that they be with Him in the same place where He is. Note, too, He did not say that He desired that His people be in heaven, but rather with Him in heaven, because that is what makes heaven, heaven. It is the very pith and marrow of heaven to be with Christ. Heaven without Christ would be an empty place for the Christian. It would lose its happiness; it would be a harp without strings, a sea without water. He desired then that we might be with Him where He is. What a prospect this is, when we will not see Him at a distance but then face-to-face! There is a sermon in those words *face-to-face*. Then we will not see Him for a little time, but

> Millions of years my wond'ring eyes
> Shall o'er Thy beauties rove,
> And endless ages I'll adore
> The glories of Thy love.[2]

If it is sweet to see Him now with the eye of faith, how sweet will it be to gaze on that blessed face forever and never have to turn one's eyes away to look on a world of weariness and woe. In heaven there will be no interruption; no weeping eyes will make us pause for a moment in our vision; no earthly joys, no sensual delights will create a discord in our melody. There we will have no fields to till, no wearied limbs,

---

2. Isaac Watts, "From Thee, My God, My Joys Shall Rise," in *Hymns and Spiritual Songs. In Three Books* (London: W. Strahan, J. and F. Rivington, J. Buckland, G. Keith, L. Hawes, W. Clarke and B. Collins, T. Longman, T. Field, and E. and C. Dilly, 1773), book 2, hymn 75 (198–99).

no dark distress, no burning thirst, no pangs of hunger, no weeping of bereavement. We will forever gaze on that Sun of Righteousness with eyes that cannot be blinded by His light and with a heart that can never be weary. Throughout a whole eternity we will realize the beating of His ever faithful heart, drink in His love, be satisfied forever with His favor, and be filled with the goodness of the Lord. The believer will receive as much of Jesus as the finite can hold of infinity. We will not then see Him for the twinkling of an eye and then lose Him, but we will see Him forever. There we will have rivers of delight and oceans of ecstatic joy. It is very hard for us to tell, with all that we can guess of heaven, how large, how deep, how high, how broad it is. None of us who has lived the nearest to our Master can form more than the faintest guess of what it is to be with Jesus where He is. And then, wrapped in the beams of His love, as a dim star is eclipsed in the sunlight, so will we sink into sweet ecstasy, which is the best description we can give of the joys of the redeemed. "Father, I *desire* that they also whom You gave Me may be *with Me* where I am." That is heaven's highest joy—to be with Christ.

Jesus's second petition is "that they may behold My glory which You have given Me." Here we have heaven's *sweetest employment.* There are many joys in heaven that will amplify the grand joy with which we started our sojourn there; meeting departed friends, along with apostles, prophets, priests, and martyrs will amplify the joy of the redeemed. But still the sun that will give the greatest light to our joy will be that we are with Jesus Christ and will behold His face. There may be other employments in heaven, but that mentioned in John 17:24 is the chief one: "that they may behold My glory." Oh, for the tongue of an angel! Oh, for the lips of cherubim for one moment to depict the mighty scenes that Christians will behold when they see the glory of their precious Master, the Lord Jesus Christ!

Think about some of the great scenes of glory that you will behold after death. The moment your soul departs from this body, you will behold the glory of Christ. The glory of His person will be the first thing that will arrest your attention. With Christ sitting in the midst of His Father's throne, your eyes will first be struck with the glory of His appearance. His person will absorb your thoughts—both His

Godhead and His manhood; the wondrous truth that He is over all, the ever-blessed God, and yet man, too, bone of our bone and flesh of our flesh.

And when for an instant you have noted this, I do not doubt that the next glory you will see will be the glory of His enthronement. Christian, you will stand at the foot of your Master's throne and look upward, and you will say, "I often used to sing on earth 'Crown him! Crown him! Crown him Lord of all!' And now I see Him!" Millions of angels bow themselves around Him. The redeemed before His throne prostrate themselves with rapture. We will take our own crowns in our hands and help to swell that solemn pomp by casting them at His feet, and we will join the everlasting song: "To Him who loved us and washed us from our sins in His blood,… to Him be glory and dominion forever and ever" (Rev. 1:5–6). Can you imagine the magnificence of the Savior? Can you conceive how thrones and princes, principalities and powers, all wait at His beck and command? It is certain, from the highest heaven to the deepest hell, that He is Lord of lords; from the remotest east to the remotest west, He is master of all. The songs of all creatures there find their focus in Him. He is the grand reservoir of praise. All the rivers of praise run into His sea, and all the hallelujahs come to Him, for He is Lord of all. This is heaven to see my Master exalted, for this has often braced me here when I have been weary and often steeled my courage when I have been faint.

And then we believers will see more glorious things yet. For we will see the glory of the final judgment. Christ, with the sound of the last trumpet, in pomp terrible and terrifying, will descend from heaven. Angels will form His bodyguard, surrounding Him on either hand. The chariots of the Lord are ten thousand times ten thousand driven by angels. The whole sky will be clad with wonders. The earth will totter at the tramp of the omnipotent King. The pillars of the heavens will stagger like drunken men beneath the weight of His eternal splendor. Heaven will display itself in the sky, while on earth all people will be assembled. The sea will give up its dead. The graves will yield their tenants from the cemetery and the battlefield. People will start to life by the thousands, and every eye will see Him, and they who crucified Him.

And while the unbelieving world will weep and wail because of Him, seeking to hide themselves from the face of Him who sits on the throne, we believers will come forward and, with songs and choral symphonies, meet our Lord. We will be caught up together with the Lord in the air, and after He has said, "Come, you blessed," we will sit on His throne; we will take our seats as assessors on that awful judgment bench. And when at the last He will say, "Depart, you cursed" and His left hand will open the door of thunder and let loose the flames of fire, we will cry, "Amen"; and when the earth will fly away and people will sink into their appointed doom, we, gladly seeing the triumph of our Master, will repeat again and again the shout of victory: "Alleluia! For the Lord God Omnipotent reigns!" (Rev. 19:6).

And to complete the scene, when the Savior ascends on high for the last time, His victories all completed and death itself being slain, you and I, attendants at His side, will shout the victor to His throne. We will behold His glory. Picture whatever splendor and magnificence you please; its reality will be far, far more than what you can think. People in this land run through the streets to see the president riding through them. They climb to their housetops to see some warrior return from battle. What a trifle! What is it to see a piece of flesh and blood bedecked with earthly power? But what will it be to see the Son of God attended with heaven's highest honors and the vast universe resounding with "Alleluia! For the Lord God Omnipotent reigns!"?

Finally, in our Savior's prayer, *heaven's greatest privilege* is also included. For we are not only to be with Christ, not only to behold His glory, but we are also to be like Christ and to be glorified with Him. Is He enthroned? So will we be. Does He wear a crown? So will we. Is He a priest and king? So will we be priests and kings to offer acceptable sacrifices forever. Mark that in all Christ has, every believer has a share. This is the sum total and the crowning of it all—to reign with Christ and to know His joy; to be honored with Him, accepted in Him, glorified with Him. This is heaven, this is heaven indeed. Live near your Master now, and when your time comes to cross the flood, you will see Him face-to-face, and only those who enjoy it every hour now can tell what that will be like.

And so with our glorification and the accompanying—yet more ultimate—glorification of Christ Himself that we will behold, we come to the moment in the execution of God's work toward which all history has been moving since the beginning of time. God will not be finally satisfied until Christ and His church are fully and finally glorified, to the praise of His Son and to the praise of His grace and His own most holy name (Phil. 2:11), and that to all eternity. All this comprises the meaning of our glorification for us Christians.

The Meaning of Our Glorification for Christ Himself

We are on holy ground when we consider the meaning of our glorification for Christ Himself. Even understood in terms of our conformity to Christ's glorious likeness and thus our arrival at our highest good, our highest good is not the ultimate divine purpose. For God's determination to conform "a great multitude which no one could number, of all nations, tribes, peoples, and tongues" (Rev. 7:9) to the likeness of His well-beloved Son was designed as a means to effect a still higher end—namely, His glorification of His Son and our Savior and messianic King. Paul teaches this when he declares that our final conformity to Christ has a more ultimate purpose, that our glorification is "that He might be the firstborn among many brethren" (Rom. 8:29). Again, Murray assists us:

> There is a final end that is more ultimate than the glorification of the people of God. It is the preeminence of Christ, and that preeminence vindicated and exemplified in the final phase of his glorification. "Firstborn" reflects on the priority and supremacy of Christ (cf. Col. 1:15, 18; Heb. 1:6; Rev. 1:5). The glory of God is always supreme and ultimate. And the supreme glory of God is manifested in the glorifying of the Son…. But the glory for the people of God is only enhanced by the emphasis placed upon the preeminence of Christ. For it is among many brethren that Christ is the firstborn. That they should be classified as brethren brings to the thought of glorification with Christ the deepest mystery of community. The fraternal relationship is subsumed under the ultimate aim of the predestinating decree. This means that the preeminence of the Son as the firstborn carries with it the correlative eminence of the children of God. The unique

dignity of the Son enhances the dignity bestowed upon the many sons who are to be brought to glory.[3]

How These Truths Influence Our Lives

These truths should *excite our desire* to attain that glory. I pray that the Holy Spirit will plant such a burning desire in your hearts for it that you will cry, "If this glory is to be had, I will have it; and I will have it God's way, for I will trust Christ and live for Him faithfully and fervently forever."

These truths should also *move us to reverent fear*. What I mean is this: if there is such a glory as we have considered in this chapter, let us tremble lest by any means we should come short of it. Even if there were no bottomless pit, no undying worm, no unquenchable fire, it would be boundless misery not to attain God's eternal glory. Let us therefore pass the time of our sojourning here watching in prayer and striving to enter in at the narrow gate.

These truths should also *move us to gratitude*. Think of this: we are going to enjoy Christ Jesus's eternal glory. What a contrast to our deserts! Shame and everlasting contempt are our rightful due apart from Christ. If we were to receive according to our merits, we should be driven from God's approving presence and from the glory of His power. Thank God He has not dealt with us according to our sins nor rewarded us according to our iniquities, but even after all our transgressions, he has still reserved us for his own eternal glory and reserved his eternal glory for us.

Finally, these truths should *move us to dauntless courage*. Knowing your destiny, should you not draw your sword and fight against sin till you have overcome it? Should you not desire to win the world for Christ and to be found finally in Him? Let us begin now to feel a holy passion for God's eternal glory, and in the strength of the Spirit and in the name of the Lord Jesus let us press forward until we reach it. Even on earth we may taste enough of this glory to fill us with delight. This glory is dawning now on earth, though its fullness will come at noontide in heaven. It sends its beams down even to our valleys and lowlands. So

---

3. Murray, "Goal of Sanctification," in *Collected Writings*, 2:316–17.

let us enjoy it now and go on singing until we reach the place where God's eternal glory will fully and finally surround us forever.

I will summarize what I have said about our glorification this way: our eternal glorification is not to be confused with the benefit that believers receive at death when their souls are made perfect in holiness and they pass immediately into glory (WSC 37). Death introduces the believer into what is termed the soul's *intermediate state*, which is certainly "gain" and "far better" than this present state (Phil. 1:21, 23). But the soul's intermediate state is not what Scripture has in mind when it speaks of the believer's eternal glory. Rather, glorification speaks of that final state into which all believers enter together at their bodily resurrection, when, being raised up in glory or transformed should they be living at Christ's return, they are openly acquitted in the day of judgment and made perfectly blessed, as coheirs with Jesus Christ, in the full enjoying of God to all eternity (WSC 38).

In light of both the sanctions of the surpassing glory that will be ours and the surpassing glory that awaits the children of God—even the consummation of our "so great salvation," all the benefits of which we are His pensioners and beneficiaries by grace alone—it seems entirely appropriate to bring our study on the application of redemption to its consummation by quoting Robert Murray McCheyne's great hymn "How Much I Owe":

> When this passing world is done,
> When has sunk yon glaring sun,
> When we stand with Christ on high
> Looking o'er life's history,
> Then, Lord, shall I fully know,
> Not till then, how much I owe.
>
> When I hear the wicked call
> On the rocks and hills to fall,
> When I see them start and shrink
> On the fiery deluge brink,
> Then, Lord, shall I fully know,
> Not till then, how much I owe.

When I stand before the throne,
Dressed in beauty not my own,
When I see Thee as Thou art,
Love Thee with unsinning heart,
Then, Lord, shall I fully know,
Not till then, how much I owe.

When the praise of heav'n I hear,
Loud as thunders to the ear,
Loud as many waters' noise,
Sweet as harp's melodious voice,
Then, Lord, shall I fully know,
Not till then, how much I owe.

Chosen not for good in me,
Wakened up from wrath to flee,
Hidden in the Savior's side,
By the Spirit sanctified,
Teach me, Lord, on earth to show,
By my love, how much I owe.

Amen and amen. May it be so, and may it be soon.

Study Questions

1. What is the eternal glory to which God has called His elect?

2. How is eternal glory described in the hymns "The Sands of Time Are Sinking" and "Jerusalem the Golden"?

3. How will glorification involve the complete salvation of the body?

4. What will the glorification of God's children mean for the rest of creation?

5. How will believers be fully conformed to Christ in their glorification?

6. What does the phrase "joint heirs with Christ" (Rom. 8:17) imply about the inheritance of the glorified saints?

7. What did Jesus say is His will for His people in His prayer of John 17:24?

8. How will the glorification of Christ's brethren be the glorification of Christ Himself?

9. How should the doctrine of glorification move us to (1) fear, (2) gratitude, and (3) courage?

10. In which of the three applications listed in the last question do you most need to grow? What are some practical steps you can take to apply the truth of glorification to this area of life?

Acknowledgment of Sources

As mentioned in the foreword, portions of this book are adapted from the following sources.

Robert L. Reymond, *A New Systematic Theology of the Christian Faith*, 2nd ed. (Grand Rapids: Zondervan, 2002), 712–801.

C. H. Spurgeon's Sermons, 63 vols. (Grand Rapids: Reformation Heritage Books, 2024–2026), including parts of the following sermons:

- Sermon #73, "Effectual Calling" (March 30, 1856)
- Sermon #1319, "The Sinner's Saviour" (October 1, 1876)
- Sermon #3121, "The Necessity of Regeneration" (November 29, 1874; published 1908)
- Sermon #1183, "Is Conversion Necessary?" (July 19, 1874)
- Sermon #3198, "What Christians Were and Are" (October 23, 1873; published 1910)
- Sermon #2556, "Life Proved by Love" (January 18, 1883; published 1898)
- Sermon #460, "Faith and Repentance Inseparable" (July 13, 1862)
- Sermon #2094, "Foundation Work" (July 7, 1889)
- Sermon #551, "Faith and Life" (January 24, 1864)
- Sermon #979, "Faith and Regeneration" (March 5, 1871)

- Sermon #1749, "A Luther Sermon at the Tabernacle" (November 11, 1883)
- Sermon #362, "None but Jesus—Second Part" (February 17, 1861)
- Sermon #213, "The Fatherhood of God" (September 12, 1858)
- Sermon #1435, "Adoption—The Spirit and the Cry" (September 22, 1878)
- Sermon #434, "Threefold Sanctification" (February 9, 1862)
- Sermon #872, "The Perseverance of the Saints" (May 23, 1869)
- Sermon #1721, "Glory!" (May 20, 1883)
- Sermon #2961, "Heirs of God" (July 22, 1875; published 1905)
- Sermon #9, "Spiritual Liberty" (February 18, 1855)
- Sermon #1892, "Why They Leave Us" (March 21, 1886)
- Sermon #188, "The Redeemer's Prayer" (April 18, 1858)